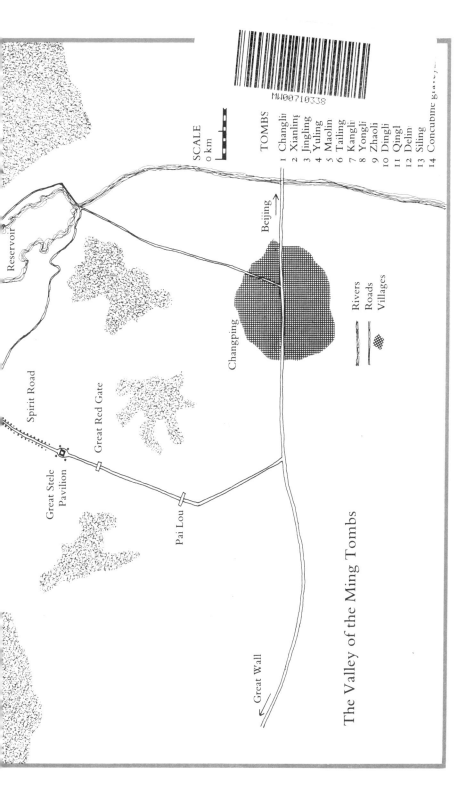

The Valley of the Ming Tombs

SCALE
0 km

Rivers
Roads
Villages

TOMBS
1 Changli
2 Xianling
3 Jingling
4 Yuling
5 Maolin
6 Tailing
7 Kangli
8 Yongli
9 Zhaoli
10 Dingli
11 Qingl
12 Delin
13 Siling
14 Concubine grav...

Reservoir

Spirit Road

Great Stele
Pavilion

Great Red Gate

Pai Lou

Great Wall

Changping

Beijing

To/ Christine Hsu
with happy memories
of my stay
in Princeton.

Ann Paludan

21 Nov. '92

IMAGES OF ASIA

The Ming Tombs

Titles in the series

Series Editors, China Titles
NIGEL CAMERON, SYLVIA FRASER-LU

The Ming Tombs

ANN PALUDAN

HONG KONG
OXFORD UNIVERSITY PRESS
OXFORD   NEW YORK
1991

Oxford University Press

Oxford   New York   Toronto
Petaling Jaya   Singapore   Hong Kong   Tokyo
Delhi   Bombay   Calcutta   Madras   Karachi
Nairobi   Dar es Salaam   Cape Town
Melbourne   Auckland

and associated companies in
Berlin   Ibadan

First published 1991
Published in the United States
by Oxford University Press, Inc., New York

British Library Cataloguing in Publication Data

Paludan, Ann 1928–
The Ming tombs.—(Images of Asia)
1. China. Tombs
I. Title II. Series
951.156
ISBN 0-19-585003-3

Library of Congress Cataloging-in-Publication Data

Paludan, Ann, 1928–
The Ming tombs / Ann Paludan.
p.   cm.—(Images of Asia)
Includes bibliographical references and index.
ISBN 0-19-585003-3 : $13.95
1. Ming Tombs (China) I. Title. II. Series.
DS793.S52465P36   1991
951'.026'092—dc20   91-13773
CIP

Printed in Hong Kong by Nordica Printing Co., Ltd.
Published by Oxford University Press, Warwick House, Hong Kong

This book is dedicated to the memory of
Dr Xia Nai
and to archaeologists all over China
in admiration of their tireless efforts to preserve the past
for the future

Contents

Acknowledgements

Figures 1.1–1.3, 1.5–1.6, 1.8–1.10, 2.1–2.2, 2.4–2.8, 3.1–3.2, 3.4, 4.1–4.3, and 5.2 were first published in Ann Paludan, *The Imperial Ming Tombs*, New Haven, Yale University Press, and Hong Kong, Hong Kong University Press, 1981, and are reproduced here with permission of Yale University Press. I am grateful to Lucy Peck, who originally drew the charts in figures 1.1, 1.2, 3.1, and 4.1.

Introduction

THE Ming Tombs are very much more than a collection of graves. The Ming is the earliest dynasty from which surface buildings on tombs have survived and here, within what the Chinese call the Valley of the Thirteen Tombs, is a unique collection of Ming architecture and stone sculpture. There are Ming towers with stele pavilions and Ming halls built in the palatial style on marble terraces; there are Ming bridges, columns, archways, and an almost perfectly preserved set of imperial stone carvings from the early fifteenth century. The lay-out of the valley, the tomb plans, and even the choice of statuary reflect contemporary Ming attitudes and philosophies. Few burial sites have preserved intact such a complete picture of their times.

The Ming dynasty was one of the great periods in Chinese history. For nearly three hundred years, from 1368 to 1644, this vast empire enjoyed peace. With a population of nearly 200 million people, it was the largest and most populous state in the world, covering an area roughly equal to that of the People's Republic of China today. Its heyday was a period of prosperity, of economic activity, and even of geographic discovery. This is the only time in Chinese history when a serious effort was made to explore by sea: the great voyages of the eunuch admiral Cheng He mapped the routes to the East Indies, India, the Persian Gulf, and the Red Sea, even reaching the coast of East Africa. Trade prospered and Western Europe started to import porcelain, which came to be known as 'china'. Painting and literature flourished and newly-found wealth was poured into building projects. The Forbidden City, the Temple of Heaven, and parts of old Beijing all date from the Ming.

The founder of the dynasty, Hongwu, was the son of poor peasants in Anhui. At an early age he was sold during a famine to a Buddhist monastery where he learned to read and write; later, he became an itinerant beggar and joined one of the many rebel bands opposed to Mongol rule. He rapidly distinguished himself as a brilliant administrator, using his victories to create unity among the rebel groups and when, in 1368, he finally ascended the Throne of Heaven as emperor, he resolved to restore the greatness of China after its years of occupation by the alien Mongols. For inspiration he turned to the past. Following the maxim 'Rule like the Tang and the Song', he reintroduced the traditional examination system of

灌注

社宗 recruitment to the administration—a system imbued with Confucianism and based on a thorough knowledge of the classics; he even revived Tang regulations governing court clothing. Above all, however, after nearly a century of neglect, he restored the role of ancestor worship at the tomb to its traditional position of importance at the heart of the imperial system.

Ancestor worship was based on a belief that the spirits of the ancestors provided a means of communication with the spirit world. The spirit of the deceased could exert an active influence on the lives of his descendants. If it were happy, it would intercede on their behalf and they would prosper, achieve high office, and have many sons. If slighted or neglected, the spirit could be spiteful, wreaking vengeance on its family. In the case of an emperor, this meant that the whole empire would suffer and the dynasty might fall.

The spirit, however, could not survive without the body; hence the importance of the tomb. The first duty of a son was to satisfy his father's spirit by building a tomb and then furnishing it with the necessities and luxuries to which the deceased had been accustomed when alive. Thereafter, he must tend to the spirit's needs by offering sacrifices and performing the rites. It was therefore advisable for a son to live near his parents' grave and for an imperial cemetery to lie within reach of the capital city.

It would be hard to overestimate the importance of a Chinese imperial tomb. Critics of funeral extravagance in the Han dynasty complained that expenditure on the great mausolea absorbed up to one third of the total annual state income. In the Tang dynasty, when whole mountains were appropriated as tumuli, the scale was even more grandiose: one mausoleum covered 182 square kilometres, the wall round another was 60 kilometres long, and the first five imperial tombs are known to have had 378 halls each.

The site of the Ming Tombs was chosen by the third emperor, the great Yongle. The first emperor, Hongwu, had his capital in Nanjing and his tomb, Xiaoling, was built in a beautiful wooded area east of the city. His successor, the second emperor, disappeared during the civil war which followed Hongwu's death and his burial place is unknown. For political and strategic reasons, Yongle moved the capital northwards to Beijing and one of his first tasks was to establish a new imperial burial ground. The move to Beijing was to be permanent and it was therefore necessary that he and his successors should be buried within easy reach of the imperial city. The problem was urgent since Yongle's wife, the empress Xu, had died before the move north and was lying in a temporary grave in Nanjing.

The choice of site was of prime importance. If the site of a tomb was misplaced, the spirit could never feel at ease. Through the centuries the Chinese had evolved a quasi-scientific theory of geomancy known as *fengshui* (literally, wind water) governing the choice of auspicious sites. This was based on the third century BC *Canon of Dwellings*, a classic which ascribed its own origins to the mythical Yellow Emperor, reputed to have lived in the twenty-seventh century BC. The system was all-embracing and it is no exaggeration to say that until the middle of this century not a house, tomb, or temple was built, not a bridge or road planned without consulting the principles of *fengshui*. It was a system open to abuse. Unscrupulous geomancers could extort a fortune from those who believed that advice on a correct site would bring them official promotion, and there has been a tendency among westerners to dismiss it as harmful superstition. Stripped of all its trappings, however, the principles of *fengshui* are based on common sense allied to a deep feeling for landscape. They provide one of the earliest and certainly one of the most successful systems of planning yet devised and it is *fengshui* which is responsible for the conscious harmonization of man and nature which distinguished classical Chinese architecture. A building should merge into the landscape, not dominate it.

The first requisite for a good site was that it should be protected from evil spirits brought by the dominant, usually northern, wind but should be open to benevolent influences from the south. Water should not run through the site—it was considered unlucky to alter the course of a stream—but should, if possible, run to the south of it. Finally, there should be a view of mountains or hills with auspicious shapes. In other words, the perfect site was very much what we would look for today: sheltered, facing south, dry but with water nearby, and with a pleasing view. It is not surprising that when the British chose the site of Government House in Hong Kong, the local Chinese commented that it was curious that a people who pretended to know nothing about *fengshui* should have chosen a site with the best *fengshui* on the island.

We know from the records that Yongle commissioned geomancers to search for an appropriate site and that he himself tried divination from tortoise shells. There is a legend that he found the final site when out hunting on his birthday. So many peasants came to wish him long life that he renamed the mountain under which he was resting 'Longevity Mountain' and decided that this must be an appropriate tomb site since imperial mausolea were always referred to as Longevity Mausolea. According to another story, twelve jade-coloured pigeons flying from the south alighted on the peak in front of him, indicating that this was the place to choose. (Birds have always been regarded as auspicious omens in China.) The flaw in this story is that there are thirteen tombs in the valley, but the last tomb was in fact built by the Qing after the fall of the Ming dynasty.

The valley eventually chosen, some 40 kilometres north-west of Beijing, answers all the requirements of *fengshui*. The northern end is protected by a shield of overlapping mountain peaks which taper gently away to east and west; the southern approach is open. The first tomb in the valley, Yongle's Changling, stands at the foot of the highest peak in the north; the tombs of later emperors were placed in the foothills to the east and west of this. In the clear winter light of north China you can see their golden roofs shining among the evergreen trees, spaced out around the northern end of the valley like points on an open fan. Flowing from west to east across the southern end of the valley are a series of small rivers and streams which are now channelled into a reservoir built in 1958. When the water level is high, the reservoir, in true classical tradition, enhances the beauty of the valley and attracts migratory wildfowl.

The emperor had chosen well. Even today, more than five hundred years after the fall of the dynasty, the valley is a place of unique charm. It has been invaded by the modern world. The tombs are a popular tourist attraction and the stately approach through the valley is often thronged with cars and tourist buses; there is a flourishing market, and even Coca Cola and hot dogs are sold in the car parks. More than five million people visit the excavated tomb, Dingling, every year; nearly as popular is Yongle's Changling, which has been restored and acts as a museum for the objects found in Dingling. But the valley has coped with this invasion. Its essential unity remains intact and as soon as you wander off the beaten track in search of one of the lesser known tombs you find yourself in a different world. The valley is fertile. These tombs, in various states of preservation, stand in the midst of fields and orchards. In spring, the green winter wheat enhances the deep red of the precinct walls; in autumn, the scene reminds you of a child's illustration of harvest time. Peasants use long bamboo poles with a muslin bag on the end to gather the brilliant orange persimmons, donkeys with paniers trot over the cobbled way with their cargo of fruit, and children glean the last of the grain from the corn fields. Each tomb has its own village, originally built to house the tomb guardians. Here the courtyards are stacked with maize or—for a short spell in November—the roofs are covered with precious winter cabbage drying before the frost.

It is a peaceful place. The tombs and villagers live in harmony according to the best principles of *fengshui*. Whilst agriculture continues outside the walls, the tombs remain deserted. Few venture inside the gates but occasionally you will find grain drying on the swept stone floor of a ruined hall; sometimes there is a shadow boxer slowly exercising among the ancient thujas or even an opera singer practising from the parapets of the stone tower with its memorial tablet. The courtyards and grassy funeral mounds attract birds: long-tailed blue magpies swoop low over the stone altars, tits and finches chatter in the trees, and there are wild flowers everywhere.

Only one tomb has been excavated. The Chinese point out that for the other tombs there is no hurry. There are so many sites, discovered accidentally during building and engineering works all over China, that demand attention. These tombs can wait for future generations to deal with. It is perhaps this feeling of the undisturbed past which gives the valley its unusual feeling of serenity. There is a magic here similar to that on Delos, where the fifth century BC Greek ruins stand on an island in which no one has been allowed to be born or to die; or in Thingvellir, untouched since the days of the great Icelandic Free State when Christianity was adopted by a majority vote in the year 1000.

I
The Tomb Plan and Architecture

THE Ming Tombs provide an unparalleled opportunity to study Chinese architecture. Here are a collection of buildings designed and constructed between the early fifteenth and mid-seventeenth centuries in a site which has since remained virtually untouched. During the fall of the Ming dynasty in 1644, rebels damaged some buildings in the north-western part of the valley but the tombs as a whole have been spared the systematic destruction which befell the great Han, Tang, and Song tombs before them.

The state of the tombs varies widely. At one end of the spectrum are two restored tombs: the halls and courtyards of Changling, the first and largest tomb in the valley, were restored to their former glory in the 1950s; and in the 1980s, the restoration of Zhaoling, the tomb of the emperor Longqing, who died in 1572, also included a reconstruction of the interior of the sacrificial hall. These restorations appear to be accurate and between them give a picture of the original state of the buildings.

Equally useful for the student of architecture, however, are the unrestored tombs. These have been cleaned up, debris and rubble having been removed, but in many the half-ruined walls are left standing, revealing the methods of construction (see colour plate 14). Overhanging eaves have fallen so that you can see the full intricacies of the complicated system whereby the heavy roofs were supported. In some tombs the buildings were decayed past saving and have been cleared away altogether leaving only the precinct walls, the marble terraces with their staircases and column bases, and the great tower housing the memorial tablet. Here you can see the tomb plan in all clarity, almost as if it were drawn in white stone on the green grass of the courtyard.

There is nothing accidental about the plan of a Chinese imperial tomb. Ancestor worship at the tomb lay at the heart of the imperial system and it was of the utmost importance that the tomb plan should satisfy the requirements posed by the rites and sacrifices. An inherent conservatism in Chinese practices meant that dynasties tended to continue the plan used by their predecessors, making only small alterations to adapt it to their own needs. The last major change in tomb design before the Ming occurred during the Han dynasty when a change in ritual in the first century led to two important additions to the basic tomb plan. Rites previously held in a temple in the city or palace were transferred to the tomb itself giving rise to a need for a sacrificial hall in which they could be held and a spirit road—an avenue of stone figures of men and animals lining the ceremonial approach from the south. Both elements became permanent features in the imperial tomb plan.

Although little remains of the Han mausolea, excavations suggest that they were fortified square enclosures on a north–south axis with gates facing the cardinal points, corner and gate towers, and short straight spirit roads. The Tang and Song developed this basic plan into a tomb city with three walled enclosures based on the plan of the imperial capital. They divided the rites into major ceremonies performed in the great sacrificial hall by the emperor or one of his family and minor rites designed to care for the more mundane needs of the deceased. The minor rites, which included the laying out of fresh clothes and water for washing and the provision of four meals a day, were carried out by resident tomb attendants, often members of the deceased emperor's family and the dowager empress. This arrangement called for dwellings within the tomb precinct and the outer enclosures were filled with minor halls and houses similar to those in the real city.

The Ming changed this. The dramatic rediscovery in the 1960s of the two earliest Ming mausolea, posthumous tombs for Hongwu's parents and grandparents, one of which had been submerged in a lake for three hundred years, shows that the Ming began by experimenting with the Tang–Song plan. They found, however, that this did not answer the requirements of their new ritual. The Ming dropped the minor rites, thus obviating the need for permanent homes inside the tomb grounds. Instead, they emphasized the importance of the major ceremonies by holding them in surroundings similar to those in the Forbidden City. They translated the ancient axiom 'Heaven round, earth square' into architectural terms. The dual nature of the tomb as a meeting place between this world and the next and its dual task—to protect the body and to satisfy the spirit—were given a quite literal expression in the tomb plan. The Ming imperial tomb was thus divided into two parts: the square (or rectangular) belonging to this world and the round belonging to the next (Fig. 1.1).

The worldly section was built like an imperial palace. Here the spirit would have felt at home. It could wander through a series of halls and courtyards decorated in the style to which it was accustomed in the Forbidden City. Chinese architecture is symmetrical: the courtyards, on a north–south axis, were flanked by low buildings along their east and west walls; the halls ran east–west at the

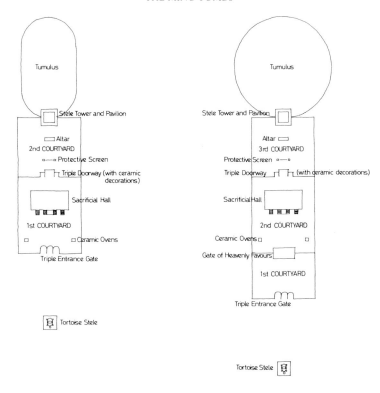

1.1 Comparison between two-courtyard and three-courtyard tombs.

northern end of the courtyard. As will be seen below, Chinese dwellings are built on the unit principle, each unit consisting of a hall set in a courtyard. Three of the Ming Tombs, Changling, Yongling, and Dingling, have three courtyards; the rest have two (Fig. 1.2). Buildings in the forecourts included dressing-rooms for the emperor and his entourage, storerooms for utensils used in the rites, and kitchens and slaughterhouses where the sacrifices were prepared. The largest hall in the third courtyard (or in two-courtyard tombs, the second), was the sacrificial hall, the Hall of Heavenly Favours, where the rites were performed. Here it can be seen how faithfully the early Ming followed the injunction to treat the dead as if they were alive. The Hall of Heavenly Favours at Changling (colour plate 7) is an almost exact replica of the largest hall in the Forbidden City, the Hall of Supreme Harmony, where the most important audiences were held. Respects were paid to the dead emperor in a simulacrum of the surroundings in which he had

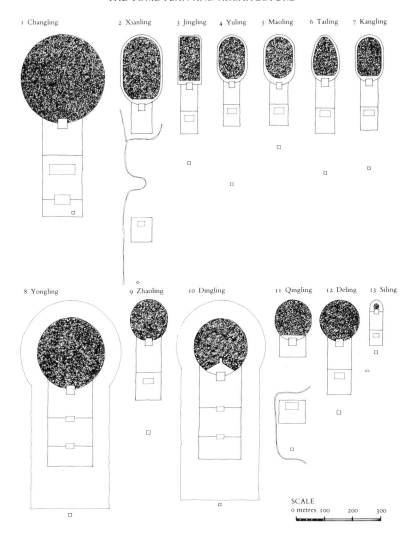

1.2 Comparative sizes of the thirteen Ming tombs.

held sway when he was alive. Until the advent of modern technology in the early part of this century, these were the two largest buildings in the whole of China.

The basic plan is the same for all the tombs. In these rectangular courtyards belonging to the 'square world', there is little to show that you are in a tomb rather than a palace. The architecture, bright colours and general arrangement are the same as in real life. Behind the sacrificial hall, however, the scene changes. The last courtyard

1.3 Protective screen, stone altar, and stele tower and pavilion, Yongling.

is dwarfed by an imposing grey stone tower on which stands a stele pavilion housing a memorial tablet or stele to the deceased (colour plate 10). Such a structure has no place in a palace courtyard; it marks the transition into the 'round heaven' of the dead.

When you pass into this courtyard, the immediate vista is blocked by a free-standing screen consisting of a pair of brightly painted wooden doors supported by two white stone columns (colour plates 11 and 15). The Ming believed that evil spirits could only travel in straight lines and this screen was designed to protect the direct access to the grave (Fig. 1.3). (Similar screens can be seen inside the street door of courtyard houses in Beijing.) Beyond this, in the shadow of the great tower, is a stone altar with replicas of the five precious objects used in the rites: two candlesticks, two flower vases, and an incense-burner. The sacrifices were always held inside the Hall of Heavenly Favours and this altar played a purely symbolic role. The Ming wished to show that they were continuing the tradition which could be traced back to pre-historical times in which it was said that 'there were no halls and sacrifices were held in the open'.

The stele tower is the most impressive feature in the whole tomb complex. Unlike the halls in their various states of decay, all the original towers and stele pavilions have survived intact. (Siling, tomb of the last emperor, never had such a tower.) The stele tower is the focus point of the whole tomb, the link between the worlds of the living and the dead. Standing at the junction of the square and the round, it belongs to both. From a distance it is the roof of the pavilion which rises above the treetops proclaiming the presence of an imperial tomb. When you stand in the courtyards, the stele tower draws the eye forward towards the grave; when you pass into the circular section and stand on the funeral mound, the stele tower dominates the skyline.

1.4 Base of tomb stele with Buddhist symbols, Deling.

The memorial tablet or stele is a simple oblong stone tablet on a square, layered base. The inscription is short, giving the name of the deceased emperor and one flattering epithet: 'wise', 'righteous', or 'virtuous'. The number of characters in the inscription is always uneven: uneven numbers belonged to *yang*, the masculine and auspicious part of the Chinese compound of two inseparable opposites known as *yin–yang*. In the early tombs, the base is decorated with geometric lotus or cloud patterns occasionally enlivened with a dragon frieze but in Deling, the last tomb in the valley to be built by the Ming, there is an unusual deviation: the base is carved with the eight Buddhist symbols (Fig. 1.4). However Buddhist an emperor might be in his private life, Buddhism had no part in Chinese burial practices and the presence of these emblems on such a monument shows how far the central system had weakened.

The second part of the tomb is reached either by a tunnel through

1.5 Unblocked tunnel through stele tower, Maoling.

the stele tower or by a steep ramp up the side of the stele tower leading to the circular fortified wall enclosing the funeral mound (Fig. 1.5). Here at last is the grave area. Beneath a large artificial tumulus—at Changling the circumference of the mound is over one kilometre long—is the underground chamber with the coffin. From the ramparts a pair of ramps lead down into the area between the stele tower and the funeral mound (Fig. 1.6). In some tombs the mound slopes gently to the foot of the tower; in others there is a half-moon courtyard behind the tower, and the southern end of the mound is formed by a stone wall in the middle of which is a final protective screen of ceramic tiles. Following ancient tradition, the mounds are wooded since trees, particularly evergreens, were believed to give sustenance to the deceased. In some tombs the original thujas have survived amongst large-leaved oaks; others have recently been replanted.

This is a different world. In the worldly courtyards all is bright colour; the eye contained by the red courtyard walls is led forward to the painted halls with their yellow roofs and dazzling white terraces. Here, apart from the green of the trees and grass, all is grey and the eye is drawn outwards to the mountains beyond. Apart from the birds, it is a place of peace and of silence. Within these grey fortifications, the dead rest undisturbed.

Whilst the tomb plan as a whole was an innovation, its components belonged to the mainstream of traditional Chinese architecture. The most striking aspect of this architecture is not its

1.6 Ramp leading from the ramparts into the area between the stele tower and the tomb mound, Maoling.

antiquity but its continuity. From earliest times, the common building material was wood. There are therefore few very old buildings in China; some thirty pre-fourteenth-century wooden buildings have been recorded. There are, however, abundant records. Our knowledge derived from historical and literary descriptions of early palace and temple construction is supplemented by clay models of houses found in Han dynasty tombs and by a few stone monumental towers placed on tombs in the first and second centuries. Although the tomb models suggest that in the Han dynasty multi-storey houses were more popular than later, clay houses have been found which are in all important respects the same as peasant houses in the north China plain nearly two thousand years later.

Houses were built as units. There was no distinction between dwelling halls and halls or temples for worship; apart from a few specific constructions such as the Temple of Heaven or pagodas (of Indian origin) and purely ornamental pavilions in parks and gardens, all buildings, large or small, private or official, palace or temple, were built on the same basic model. The unit consisted of a single-storey hall in a rectangular courtyard on a north–south axis. The hall, placed at the northern end of the courtyard faced south; that is to say, the building ran east–west with doors and windows on the south and the other three walls blank. Additional buildings of minor importance could flank the east and west sides of the

1.7 Interior of the Hall of Heavenly Favours, Changling, with *nanmu* columns.

courtyard but, apart from the protective screen just inside the main entrance, the southern part of the courtyard was always left clear. The difference between a peasant's house and a palace lay in the size and number of units and in their decoration. A large house or, as we have seen above, a palace, consisted of a series of connected units with halls of increasing height.

The methods of construction appear to have remained equally constant. All dwellings, large or small, were made up of three elements: a foundation, a wooden framework, and a roof. The foundation of rammed earth was raised to keep the building dry. In grander buildings, this earthen base was transformed into a series of marble terraces of great beauty with elegant balustrades and staircases. The framework consisted of a set of wooden columns placed evenly in rows, creating what were known as 'bays' between them. These columns carried the roof and the size of a hall depended on their number and height. Whereas a small house rested on four wooden posts, the Hall of Heavenly Favours at Changling has sixty columns in four rows, each column made from a single tree-trunk nearly 13 metres high (Fig. 1.7).

The walls are merely infilling made from earth and straw, brick and rubble. Behind the plaster in the half-ruined halls of the unrestored tombs, you can see the closely packed small stones and earth, and the gaps in which the wooden columns once stood. The stone column bases have survived and there are ventilation holes with decorative grids in the walls to protect the wood from humidity (colour plate 14 and Fig. 1.8).

1.8 Part of the stele pavilion, Deling. The supporting wooden beam can be seen through a gap in the plaster below a ventilation hole.

Since the walls were perishable, they had to be protected from rain; hence the development of the distinctive Chinese roof with its overhanging eaves and elaborate roof supports. All the fantasy in a Chinese building is concentrated in the roof. The roofs in the Ming Tombs belong to the northern style where the swing of the eaves is less pronounced than in the south but, even here, the overhanging eaves give lightness. The height of the roof indicated the importance of a building and the major halls had double roofs. Beneath the eaves, the complicated bracket system needed to support the heavy roof was turned into a decorative feature, painted in bright colours (Fig. 1.9). Further decoration was provided by the ceramic beasts,

1.9 Restored double roof of Dingling stele pavilion.

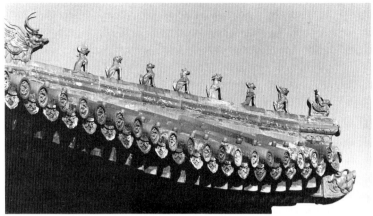

1.10 Ceramic roof animals, Changling.

each made from a single tile. In its wide mouth a *qiwen*, one of the sons of the dragon who was fond of water, holds the main roof beam to protect it from fire; on the four corners of the eaves sit a row of mythical creatures (Fig. 1.10).

It is a simple system, effective and very flexible. The resulting house or hall was dry and draught-proof. The design made good use of the climate: in winter, the low sun shines in through the southern windows; in summer, the eaves keep the interior cool and life is carried on in the courtyard. It is a cheap system. As with modern pre-fabricated housing, there is no need for an architect since the house could be ordered by specifying the number and height of the beams. The building would not last for ever—the wood might rot or catch fire—but it was easy to rebuild an identical building. (The Chinese date a building from its original construction taking little note of latter reconstructions.)

The basic unit, as we have seen, was not a building but a building in a courtyard. In the Ming Tombs, it is possible to study the relationship between the two and it becomes clear that the proportions were carefully designed to produce a desired effect. The main courtyard in Changling is so large, the terraces on which the Hall of Heavenly Favours stands are so wide, that the hall itself looks deceptively low. It is only when you stand on the terraces and look down at the buildings round about that you appreciate its true height. In the next courtyard, exactly the opposite result is produced. There the height of the stele tower is exaggerated by the relatively short length of the courtyard.

The building might be plain, almost boring in form but it is brought to life by its surroundings, by the beautiful marble terraces, by the flowers and trees in the courtyard, and by the use of colour. Chinese architecture is unusual in that colour is recognized as an integral part of a building. There were strict rules about colour, some of which went back to the Bronze Age. The Han *Book of Rites*, a chronicle of Zhou dynasty customs, states that 'the pillars of the Son of Heaven are red' and it has been confirmed by archaeologists that red mercuric oxide was used as a wood preservative as early as the eleventh century BC. Each part of an imperial building had its prescribed colour: tiles were yellow; terraces, staircases, and bridges, white; courtyard walls were red whilst woodwork such as roof brackets, window and door frames, and ceilings were polychrome with blue, green, and gold predominating. In this way, the originally functional unit was given contrast and the final result, seen at its best in the Forbidden City and the Ming Tombs, produces an extraordinary harmony between the building and its surroundings.

In the round grave area, quite another method of construction was used. Above ground, as we have seen, the tower and ramparts were made of unadorned grey stone. Below ground everything was of white marble or stone. The construction of the underground chamber is considered in detail in Chapter 4 but it is worth noting here the deliberate contrast in construction methods between the two parts of the tomb. In the square 'world', worldly methods, perishable and renewable, were used; in the round 'heaven', all was built for eternity.

2

The Approach

DURING the Ming dynasty, when the burial grounds were in active use, the journey from the capital took two days. The passage of the emperor and his entourage of over a thousand attendants was a serious affair; roads were swept, bridges repaired, and lodgings prepared for the two nights spent en route. Today, the trip takes less than an hour and the first sign that you are approaching the tombs comes as a surprise. The road makes a bend and then, suddenly, towering above you, is what is said to be the largest ceremonial archway in China (colour plate 1). The archway stands on the central north–south axis through the valley and, in winter, when the air is clear, you can see through the central archway to the Great Red Gate and the Great Stele Pavilion; the three monuments lead in a straight line to the distant roofs of Yongle's Changling.

Wooden memorial archways or *pai lou* like this have a long history and can still be seen throughout China. They were a recognition of merit, erected on imperial orders, but often paid for by the inhabitants of a village or town wishing to honour a distinguished administrator or a virtuous widow who had resisted the temptation to remarry. The woodwork was always brightly painted and a typical example can be seen outside the main entrance to the Summer Palace in Beijing.

The Ming Tombs' *pai lou* is a masterpiece of carving. The archway, 33.6 metres wide and 10.5 metres tall, consists of six columns, each made from a single block of stone. The stone roof is an exact reproduction of a wooden roof with all its intricate crossbeams and supports, and the tablet above the central opening, which would normally carry an inscription, is left blank since it was not fitting that inferiors should write about the Son of Heaven. The column bases are carved with fabulous beasts chosen for their symbolism: on the panels of the outer columns two lions, symbols of strength, play with the Buddhist 'night-shining pearl'; on the second and fifth column panels are *makara*, a mythical creature of Indian origin symbolizing fertility, and on the central pair, magnificent five-clawed dragons, symbols of the emperor (Fig. 2.1). Above the panels are more fabulous creatures carved in the round. On the outer, second and fifth columns, these are lions; on the central pair, the mythical *qilin*. The *qilin* had an ancient and impeccable pedigree, having been seen just before the birth of Confucius.

2.1 Base of a *pai lou* column with an imperial dragon and a fabulous *qilin*.

It symbolized good government and wisdom, appearing only when a sage sat on the throne, and its peaceful nature was shown by the fact that its horns were soft. (Early *qilin* had only one horn which led to its name being translated as unicorn, but this, as can be seen, is misleading.) From the first, the Ming wished to emphasize the traditional, Chinese nature of their rule, based on Confucian ideas of good government and harmony in contrast to the hated and often arbitrary rule of the Mongols who preceded them. For this reason, the *qilin* appears more often than any other creature in Ming tomb decoration; its presence assured the onlooker that the empire was well run and at peace.

Strictly speaking, this archway is outside the tomb precincts. The *pai lou* was erected in 1540 by the eleventh emperor, Jiajing, when the burial grounds had already been in use for more than a century. The previous emperor had no sons and Jiajing, descended from a younger brother, was anxious to show that his lineage was as good as that of his predecessors. As well as adding monuments to the approach, he designed his own tomb, Yongling, on a scale greater than that of Changling, hitherto the largest tomb in the valley, and used materials of a finer quality.

The official entrance to the tomb grounds was the Great Red Gate one kilometre north of the *pai lou*. The central arch was reserved for the passage of a dead emperor; living emperors used the eastern opening; lesser ranks entered on the west. Outside the gate, there used to stand a 'dismount tablet' (*xia ma men*) ordering all who passed by to dismount from their horses. The penalty even in Qing times for disobeying this edict was 'one hundred blows with the long [bamboo] stick'. Inside the gate on the east there was originally a large pavilion with three hundred apartments where the emperor and his attendants rested after the long journey and changed their clothes.

There were still another 5 kilometres to go. The way from here to Changling is marked by a series of monuments and statuary known as the spirit road, since it led to the spirit's new abode in the underground grave. This approach served the entire valley. In

2.2 South face of the great memorial stele.

other dynasties each ruler had his own set of monuments lining the way to his tomb, and the valley of the Ming Tombs is the only imperial burial ground in which all mausolea are served by a single spirit road. The avenue leads up the central axis of the valley, pointing towards the highest peak in the north beneath which lay Changling. Later tombs were connected to the central avenue by side roads rather like the branches of a tree, but apart from their small memorial tablets or stelae on tortoise bases, there were no individual approach monuments (colour plate 12).

Half a kilometre north of the Great Red Gate is a red pavilion housing a memorial stele serving the whole dynastic burial ground. The importance of the pavilion with its double roof is emphasized by four very beautiful flanking columns or *hua biao*, erected in the same year as the *pai lou* by Jiajing.

The stele is an almost exact replica of the largest stele in China, that on the tomb of the first Ming emperor in Nanjing. The slab, some 10 metres high, is carved in one piece with its base, an enormous tortoise 4.5 metres long, 2.5 metres wide and nearly 2 metres tall (Fig. 2.2). The shape of the stele and its decoration hark back to the first century when such memorial tablets were first made in stone. Before this, stelae were wooden and used to support the heavy coffin as it was lowered into the grave. (A tablet with a hole in it was set up at each end of the grave and a rope for manoeuvring the coffin was threaded through the hole.) The earliest stone stelae retained the hole but, apart from this detail, the design and decoration of such memorial tablets remained unchanged through the centuries. This tablet is crowned with hornless dragons (*li*) who would shower blessing on the deceased's descendants; the tortoise bearing the tablet was a *ba xia*, one of the nine sons of the dragon who was famous for its ability to carry weights. Its rounded shell symbolized the vault of the sky and its belly the earth moving on the waters. All the tortoises in the Ming valley stand on a base carved with waves and sea creatures (Fig. 2.3).

The dedication on the south side of the stele is to Yongle's mausoleum, Changling of the Great Ming Dynasty. The inscription of 3,500 characters was composed by Yongle's son, the emperor Hongxi, in 1425 and written by the renowned calligrapher Cheng Nanyao, but the stele was not erected until 1436. On the reverse face is a poem by the Qing emperor, Qianlong, in which he devotes one line to each of the tombs in the valley. The small memorial stelae marking the approach to each of the later tombs carried an inscription giving the name of the deceased in the form: 'Spirit road leading to the tomb of. . . .'.

2.3 Prawn and waves on the stone base of the tortoise stele, Dingling.

Like the *pai lou* and the memorial stele, the *hua biao* are stone editions of wooden architectural features dating back to very early times. Winged columns like this signalled the entrance to government buildings and places of importance; rubbings of Han dynasty tomb bricks from the first and second centuries show *hua biao* outside the gates of large houses and at each end of a bridge. These Ming Tombs columns are exactly the same as those at the southern entrance to the Forbidden City in Beijing and their decoration shows the dragon in all its glory (Fig. 2.4).

In the west, the dragon is evil—St George slew the dragon. For the Chinese the reverse was true. The dragon, equally at home in the watery deep or rain-giving clouds, was the source of all life. Without rain nothing could grow. The powers of the dragon soared above those of all other mythical creatures and it was natural that it should symbolize the emperor. (The earliest historical dynasty, the Xia, whose rule ended in the seventeenth century BC used the dragon as their emblem.) During the Ming dynasty there were clearly delimited categories of dragons: the five-clawed *long* was reserved for the emperor; lesser members of the imperial family had to make do with the four-clawed *mang*.

The columns are guarded by fabulous creatures on lotus bases. (Although the lotus motif was of Indian origin, brought to China with Buddhism, it had long been assimilated into the general reper-

2.4 One of the four *hua biao* columns surrounding the stele pavilion.

toire of Chinese art forms and had lost its religious significance.)
The southern pair face south, bidding welcome to visitors coming
to pay their respects at the tombs; the northern pair face north,
reminding those who leave to come again soon. These animals
have various names, the most expressive of which is 'Roaring towards the Sky' but perhaps the most common is *qilin* like the beasts
on the central arch of the *pai lou*.

Fabulous beasts in China played a very different role from their
western counterparts. Their existence was recognized in imperial
regulations and their symbolism was a question for discussion at
the highest levels. When in the west we wish to create beings with
supernatural powers, we tend to give them human form: witches,
fairies, wizards, elves, or gnomes. In China, they were given animal form. Animals were believed to be media for contacting the spirit
world and all the helpers of the fabled Queen Mother of the West,
who ruled the land of the immortals, were animals. Through the
centuries a vast menagerie of creatures came into being, their super-

natural qualities indicated by a series of easily recognizable features: wings, horns, flame patterns, scales, and even an outstretched tongue. Just as in the west a fairy is equally efficient whether she appears in a black cloak with a broomstick or in a ballet skirt with a wand, these Chinese creatures assumed many guises. The same beast could have many names; the same name could cover many forms. What mattered was that its appearance should convey its special abilities to the viewer. The many *qilin* in the Ming Valley are by no means all alike but they bear a family resemblance and their symbolism remains constant.

Beyond the stele pavilion begins an avenue of stone figures of men and animals lining the spirit road (colour plate 2). The practice of providing the dead with a stone guard of honour to replace the living guard they would have enjoyed in life began in the Han dynasty. Like the living guard, these stone figures played a dual role. By their content and number they proclaimed the status of the deceased, the number and subject matter of the statuary being regulated according to the rank of the deceased. At the same time they protected the grave. Animals, as we have seen, were endowed with supernatural powers which, since they were invisible, were as effective against evil spirits as against worldly wrongdoers. The Chinese believed that a statue had inherent powers to bring about that which it represented: the stone statue of an official would, by its very existence, improve the quality of the administration; the statue of a tiger would deter tomb robbers, not by its fierce appearance but because the creation of the figure would call its tiger-like qualities into existence. The content of the statuary was therefore chosen carefully for its symbolism and each dynasty devised a new pattern expressing the message which it wished to give to the world. Earlier dynasties such as the Tang and the Song had used the spirit road to recreate worldly occasions in which stone horses and grooms stood as if on parade or awaiting an imperial audience. The Ming adopted a much more symbolic approach. They made no attempt to reproduce reality and chose their subjects to present the different aspects of the Ming empire as the Ming emperors wished it to be seen.

The avenue is one of the most popular places in the whole valley. Families crowd round the animals photographing each other and there is a flourishing market in the large parking place behind the eastern row of figures. The number of tourists is so great that it has become necessary to fence the statues in, to prevent damage by the crowds. There are plans to move motor traffic away from the avenue and, if you have time, it is worth walking away from the

1. Ceremonial archway (*pai lou*), erected by the emperor Jiajing in 1540.

2. Spirit road with a standing *qilin* in the foreground.

3. Fabulous *xiezhi*, symbol of justice (height 1.9m) on the spirit road.

4. President of one of the Six Boards (height 3.2m) on the spirit road.

5. Grand Secretary (height 3.2m) on the spirit road.

6. Archway of the Dragon and Phoenix Gate.

7. Hall of Heavenly Favours, Changling.

8. Triple marble terraces, Changling.

9. Sacrificial oven for burning paper and silk, Changling.

10. Stele tower and pavilion, and altar with the set of five objects used during the rites, Zhaoling.

11. Protective screen in front of the Triple Doorway into the second courtyard, Jingling. The connecting courtyard wall and halls have been cleared away.

12. Tortoise stele marking the way to Kangling.

13. Stele tower and pavilion, Yongling. The sacrificial hall has been cleared away leaving the terraces bare.

14. Stele tower and pavilion, Yuling. In the foreground are the walls of the sacrificial hall with the emplacements of the original supporting beams (which have now rotted away).

15. View from the stele tower over courtyards with altar and protective screen, Yongling.

16. Ramparts at Maoling with the roof of Yuling stele pavilion in the distance.

car park, back to the southern, uncrowded end of the alley where you can get some idea of how it would originally have looked.

The avenue starts with a pair of columns carved like beacons. Known as *wang zhu* or 'look towards' columns, they light the road for the wandering spirit to find its way back to its underground abode; at the same time the heat of their flames offers it nourishment. The shaft is carved with clouds and a dragon peers through the smoke at the top.

There follow twelve pairs of stone animals and six pairs of stone men. Each pair of animals appears twice, first sitting and then standing, and it is said that at midnight the pair which have been resting change places with those on guard nearest to the emperor. The animals are a mixture of real and fantastic and come in the following order: lions, *xiezhi*, camels, elephants, *qilin*, and horses. The real animals are, or were, all native to China and denote the extent of the empire: horses from the western steppes, elephants from the tropical regions in the south, and camels, still a familar sight bearing coal to Beijing in the early 1970s, from the north. Elephants were used in Ming imperial ceremonies and a special palace was built for them in 1495. The Qing continued to use them until 1884 when one went beserk, throwing an old deaf woman over the rootops and tossing a donkey into a shop. After this, the elephants were in disgrace and left to die slowly of malnutrition.

These statues are large—the elephants nearly 3.5 metres high—and carved in monumental style. Unlike western sculptures, these figures were not carved as works of art; nor were they intended to be judged individually and from all angles. The aim of the sculptor was to impress those coming to perform the rites—people walking in a procession with their eyes forward and slightly down—with the essential characteristics and properties of the animal. In the Tang and Song dynasties horses were carved as they would have been on parade, with fine saddle-cloths and bells round their necks, and with grooms. Stone elephants in the Song and Qing dynasties wear embroidered saddles and are accompanied by Indian mahouts or bear elaborate vases on their backs. When the Ming first came to power they adopted the Tang and Song approach: horses on the mausolea of the first emperor's parents and grandparents are harnessed and with grooms. Once the dynasty was established, however, it worked out its own definitive pattern of statuary based on a purely symbolic approach in which there was no scope for such realism. None of the animals in the Ming Tombs have attendants; none, except for the lions with their apparently inalienable collar, wear man-made trappings.

The fabulous beasts describe the nature of Ming government: the *qilin* stood for good administration and peace, the lion for military strength and security, and the *xiezhi* for justice. The *xiezhi* was as ancient as the *qilin*; it was said to be white and to roar when it saw injustice (colour plate 3). *Xiezhi* had been embroidered on the hats of judges in the third and fourth centuries and were worn on the badges of imperial censors under the Ming. Unlike the tiger, which was a familiar beast in China, the lion was not indigenous and was considered a fabulous beast. The first examples had been brought to the imperial menageries as tribute in the first century, and the lion entered the Chinese animal world by virtue of its similarities to the tiger. Like the tiger, it symbolized strength and power; the only difference between first- and second-century stone lions and tigers is that the former have stylized manes. (The playing lions on the *pai lou* base hark back to these early felines.) With the advent of Buddhism, however, a new type of lion arrived—the Buddhist guardian. By the late seventh century this creature had ousted the earlier tiger-type and from the late seventh century onwards all lions carved in the round took the form with which we are familiar today: these were the predecessors of the myriad lions seated out-

2.5 Seated lion in the spirit road.

26

side Chinese official buildings all over the world. Once again, however, this lion had little if any contact with the real animal. Its pose showed that it was at the service of man. It symbolized power and security but, as the centuries passed, its appearance became more and more artificial. With trinkets dangling from its collar and an increasingly elaborate hairstyle, it was quite clearly a creature of fantasy (Fig. 2.5).

The stone officials represent the highest offices of state. There are two pairs of military generals: the first pair hold a baton, symbol of military command (Fig. 2.6); the second pair stand with hands clasped in front of them. These are followed by four pairs of civil officials. From their clothing it has been possible to establish that the first two pairs represent Presidents of the Six Boards (colour plate 4) whilst the second two pairs are Grand Secretaries (colour plate 5). The administration of the Ming empire was divided into six boards, responsible for personnel, revenue, rites, war, justice, and works. Presidents of these boards were the highest figures in the administration, not unlike ministers in western countries. The Grand Secretaries had no specific administrative duties. They were, however, the emperor's closest advisers and their pre-eminence is

2.6 Military commander with baton in the spirit road (height 3.2m).

recognized by the fact that they stand in the place of honour nearest to the ruler. All four pairs carry the *hu*, a tablet used by senior officials during an imperial audience. With heads bowed, they held the tablet in front of them to note the imperial commands.

Giving these figures a hurried glance, westerners often dismiss them as stiff and lifeless. Contrasting the impassive faces with the more lively and individualistic expressions they are accustomed to in western statuary, they decide that these are poor sculptures, of little interest. This is a misconception. The aim of the sculptor in creating these stone officials was the same as that with the animals: to produce an image possessing certain qualities. The sculptor's purpose was practical; his task was to present to the world a picture of virtuous and able officials and by so doing to strengthen the imperial system. His work was judged not on any abstract ideas of beauty but on its ability to achieve this result. This approach produced a result almost diametrically opposite to that sought in the west. The Chinese sculptor strove to capture those abstract qualities such as virtue, wisdom, strength of purpose, and serenity which the ideal official should possess. In this context, individual characteristics had no place and would merely distract the viewer. What the westerner finds most displeasing was thus what the Chinese most prized.

The officials in the Ming Tombs represent the peak of abstraction in Chinese stone portraiture; these dignified figures stand for the office, not the holder, and it is as if a fine veil has been drawn between them and reality.

There is a marked contrast between the uniformity of the facial expressions and the detail with which the costumes are carved. It was by a man's clothing and emblems of office that his rank was known; to produce the correct effect, every detail needed to be accurate, so that these provide reliable three-dimensional examples of ceremonial dress in the early fifteenth century. The robes are archaistic. This is not what was worn in the street during the Ming dynasty. In his efforts to re-establish continuity with the great imperial past, the first emperor had revived certain Tang clothing regulations for court use. As in the robes worn at a British coronation or by beefeaters at the Tower of London, these Ming costumes are inherited from earlier times with a few adaptations such as the use of Mandarin squares to denote rank.

Chinese sculptors excel in reproducing one material in another and when you examine these sculptures closely you can almost feel the different textures: the knotted ropes, metal belt clasps, or winged ear pieces, the leather overskirts, jade pendants, and silk embroidered panels. The costumes are filled with symbolism: according to the imperial clothing regulations, different animals were used to symbolize different military ranks whilst birds denoted the civil distinctions. A mythical horned beast holds the warrior's belt in its mouth; another forms the lower part of the epaulette; galloping horses on the overskirt stand for military vigilance (Fig. 2.7). The back panels of the civilians are embroidered with the cranes prescribed for the two highest civilian ranks (Fig. 2.8).

Beyond the officials, the way is apparently blocked. Across the central axis is an elegant free-standing triple gate and the road to the tombs is forced to branch round it, continuing again on the far side. The purpose of this gate was, as we have seen, to protect the deceased from straight-flying evil spirits. Sometimes called the 'Star-lintelled Gate' (*ling xing men*), or 'Lattice gate', it is more popularly known as the 'Dragon and Phoenix Gate' because of its role in protecting the imperial graves. The framework is of white stone; the doorposts have wings similar to those on the *hua biao* and are guarded by long-haired *qilin* (colour plate 6). The doors would have been wooden.

From here Changling is visible in the foothills to the north. The scene for the tombs has been set. The series of approach monuments create a picture of the magnificence and might of the Ming

2.7 Back of commander's robe with **galloping horses** symbolizing military vigilance.

29

2.8 Back of robe embroidered with cranes, President of one of the Six Boards.

dynasty. The great marble *pai lou* proclaimed that this was a burial ground of no ordinary stature; the stele, with its surrounding columns reaching for the sky, revealed the identity of the deceased; the avenue of statues announced the extent of their domain and the nature of their government. The message was clear: this was a great dynasty whose territory ranged from northern deserts and steppes to tropical regions; it was governed with justice and wisdom; it was at peace and militarily secure under the administration of wise and able officials. Above all, it was unified. The valley forms a self-contained unit: this is China 'within the wall'.

3
Changling

CHANGLING, tomb of the great Yongle, the third Ming emperor, who moved the capital north to Beijing, was built in the early years of the fourteenth century. Its construction was contemporaneous with that of the Forbidden City but whereas the palaces in the latter were extensively restored and added to by the Qing, Changling has preserved its original form. Restored in the 1950s, it is the oldest and most perfect example of a self-contained Ming palatial complex.

The tomb is placed in the foothills so that the last stretch of the great approach across the valley leads uphill. The tomb precincts are enclosed by a high red wall roofed with yellow tiles indicating that this was an imperial area. (Only the emperor might use yellow tiles; buildings for lesser ranks had to make do with green.) The entrance in the centre of the southern wall is as imposing as that of an imperial palace. Passing through one of the side openings—the central archway is barred as it would have been in imperial times—you find yourself in another world. This is a world of fantasy and colour; here is Chinese architecture as one always imagined it would be. The courtyards are filled with flowers: plum blossom in early spring, followed by the great pink and red peonies of which the Chinese are so fond; later come the chrysanthemums. Trees are trained into unusual shapes and, in winter, provide decoration with their shadows. The buildings are a blaze of colour: double roofs of glowing yellow stand out against the blue northern sky, brilliantly painted halls of ascending height stand on dazzling white terraces, and a small pavilion set amidst fruit trees is surrounded by white marble balustrades. Three paved ways lead due north to the Gate of Heavenly Favours directly in front of you.

The pavilion in the south-east corner of the courtyard is a Qing addition, housing a stele erected on 30 December 1659 by order of the first Qing emperor, Shunzhi. The Manchu Qing, who followed the Ming, were a non-Han people from the north-east. Realizing the advantages bestowed by legitimacy, they were, from the first, anxious to impress the Chinese that they were the rightful heirs to the Mandate of Heaven, not foreign usurpers. They adopted the Chinese traditions of ancestor worship at the tomb and maintained, as far as was practical, the full panoply of Chinese burial practices, including that of showing respect for the tombs of earlier Chinese emperors. Not only did they give the last Ming

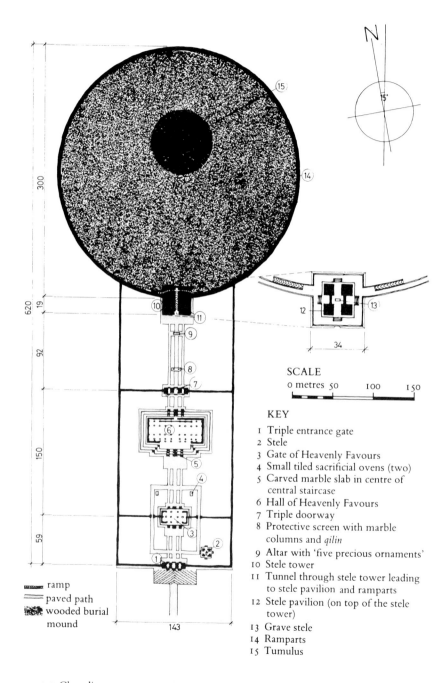

N

15°

SCALE

0 metres 50   100   150

KEY

1 Triple entrance gate
2 Stele
3 Gate of Heavenly Favours
4 Small tiled sacrificial ovens (two)
5 Carved marble slab in centre of central staircase
6 Hall of Heavenly Favours
7 Triple doorway
8 Protective screen with marble columns and *qilin*
9 Altar with 'five precious ornaments'
10 Stele tower
11 Tunnel through stele tower leading to stele pavilion and ramparts
12 Stele pavilion (on top of the stele tower)
13 Grave stele
14 Ramparts
15 Tumulus

ramp
paved path
wooded burial mound

3.1 Changling.

emperor, who had hanged himself during the fall of Beijing in 1644, a proper burial and tomb in the Ming valley but they appointed a member of the Ming imperial family to be in charge of the Ming burial grounds and to perform the necessary rites at the tombs of his ancestors. Money was allotted to repair tombs which had been damaged by rebels during the fall of the dynasty and this stele is inscribed with three edicts, from 1659, 1786, and 1804, referring to repairs to Changling and prescribing penalties for those who felled timber within the tomb area. The style of the stele and its tortoise base is more ornate than that of the Ming stele in the spirit road. The dragon ancestry of the tortoise is made explicit: it has a raised, ridged spine, two horns, and feet with five claws. Instead of the customary neatly twined hornless dragons or *li*, the crown of the tablet is protected with a large serpentine dragon with a raised head and two prominent horns.

This first courtyard and the Gate of Heavenly Favours form a sort of antechamber not unlike the hall in a stately home. The gate has a single roof and five bays; its name, *ling en men*, is painted on a wooden tablet hanging above the central opening on the south (Fig. 3.2). The three central bays are open to both sides creating a kind of reception hall; the closed bays on the east and west formed rooms in which the emperors and his officials made the final adjustments to their clothing before proceeding to the sacrificial hall. The coffered ceiling is painted in blue, green, red, and gold.

3.2 Name tablet and wooden roof brackets, Gate of Heavenly Favours (*ling en men*), Changling.

The next courtyard is one of the great triumphs of Chinese architecture. There is a feeling of spaciousness and light; the relationship between the proportions of the courtyard and those of the great Hall of Heavenly Favours at its northern end creates an extraordinary impression of harmony (colour plate 7). The building and its surroundings are at one. This was the heart of the worldly section of the tomb, corresponding to the great courtyard and Hall of Supreme Harmony in the Forbidden City. It was here that the rites were performed in which the living emperor paid his respects to the spirits of his ancestors and sought their blessings for himself, his dynasty, and his realm.

As you enter the courtyard, the way is flanked by two small ceramic ovens formed like miniature imperial halls (colour plate 9): stone foundations, wooden trellis windows, and overhanging roof are all reproduced in yellow and green ceramic tiles. Here silk and paper money and messages were burned during the sacrifices in order to transform them into a medium more easily acceptable to the spirits. The roof, for once at eye level, is a good place to examine the small animals which guard the eaves of Chinese palaces. Each creature is made from a single tile with the section of roof ridge on which it sits. The animals are taken from a series: dragon, phoenix, lion, *qilin*, and winged horses; the number depends on the size of the building but is always uneven and never exceeds eleven. This use of a fixed series was a Ming innovation and is only found in the Beijing area. Earlier dynasties enjoyed a greater freedom of choice which can still be found away from the capital. Indeed, the further south you go in China, the more ornate roof decorations become, until their ridges and eaves are a veritable forest of animals, real and imaginary, heroes from legends, and warriors.

Many differing explanations are given for the Ming roof animals. Modern guides tend to dismiss them as pure ornamentation but, given the deeply symbolic approach of Ming decoration, it seems likely that they have a historical background. One popular theory is that they commemorate an incident from the third century BC: the man sitting on a chicken at the lower end of the eave is the wicked Prince Min of the state of Qin, who in 283 BC was strung from the corner of a roof and left to die. His weight prevents the chicken from flying down to the ground whilst his way back up the roof is guarded by the animals behind him. The larger horned head at the upper end of the row is, like the creature holding the upper roof ridge, the fire-quelling son of the dragon, the *qiwen* (see Fig. 1.10).

The Hall of Heavenly Favours is the largest surviving ancient hall in China. As we have seen, the Ming took seriously the injunction to treat the dead as if they were alive and this hall was built according to the plans for the Hall of Supreme Harmony in the Forbidden City. The Beijing hall was started in 1407, that of Changling in 1409, but the former had to be completely rebuilt after a disastrous fire in 1545. These halls were designed and erected at the height of Ming power. As ruler of the most populous nation on earth, Yongle was determined that his new capital should reflect the might and glory of his empire, and the palaces in the Forbidden City, the Temple of Heaven, and Changling can hold their own with the world's greatest architecture.

The exterior of the Hall of Heavenly Favours has been fully restored. The roof and painted wooden roof supports are in excellent condition and the only visible modern alteration is that the window panes are of glass rather than paper. Once again the name—*ling en dian*—on a tablet above the central doorway on the south, proclaims the purpose of the building. Here the spirit received the respects and offerings of its descendants and, satisfied, rewarded them with heavenly favours.

The glory of this hall lies in its terraces (colour plate 8). These are

3.3 Baluster carved with phoenix, Changling.

the oldest set of triple terraces in China, predating those of the Forbidden City and the Temple of Heaven. They rise in tiers, each with its open-work balustrades and posts carved with dragons and phoenixes against a background of clouds. The artists have been given free rein and there is a delightful variety of poses (Fig. 3.3). The five-clawed dragon, symbol of the emperor, is of course *yang*; the phoenix, symbol of the empress, has only four claws, even numbers belonging to the female *yin*. Water-spouts at each corner are carved with dragon-head gargoyles similar to those in the Forbidden City and the Temple of Heaven. A triple staircase, 7 metres high, leads to the main entrance into the hall. Up the centre of the central staircase is a beautiful marble carpet with a patterned border which would originally have been painted red (Fig. 3.4). In the lower part, two winged horses canter across mountains and waves denoting the sea; above them, three pairs of large dragons disport among the clouds. When the emperor came to the hall, he was carried over this slab in a palanquin, whilst his officials used the side staircases. Similar carved slabs in later tombs in the valley are on a more modest scale and, from Yongling onwards, show the phoenix playing with the dragon. (The last dowager-empress of the Qing dynasty, Ci Xi, who died in 1908 having effectively ruled China for some fifty years, proclaimed her power by having the phoenix carved above the dragon on the slab leading to her sacrificial hall.)

Restoration of the interior of the hall has been limited to the

3.4 Marble carpet up the central staircase leading to the Hall of Heavenly Favours, Changling.

structure: the floor, wall, and painted, coffered ceiling of the hall have been refurbished and the pillars remain in all their splendour. The hall, 66.75 × 29.31 metres, is nine bays wide and five bays deep. The roof is held by sixty columns nearly 13 metres high, the largest four of which have a diameter of 1.17 metres (see Fig. 1.7). Seven metres from the northern wall, a screen nearly reaching the ceiling hides a single exit to the north. Each column, on a round stone base, is made from a single trunk of *machilus nanmu*, a tree from south-west China prized for the colour and scent of its wood. Matteo Ricci, the great Jesuit who was the first westerner ever to set foot in the Forbidden City, has described meeting a load of such tree-trunks on the Grand Canal in the early part of the seventeenth century. He was told that they were destined for the capital to re-build one of the palaces of the emperor Wan Li which had burned down. The trunks were bound with ropes and pulled by many thousand men; the convoy stretched for nearly 4 kilometres and Ricci reckoned that the total journey from Sichuan to Beijing would take some three years.

The hall has seen many changes. Sir Reginald Johnston, tutor to the last emperor of China, has recorded that a descendant of the Ming, the Marquis of Zhu, continued to officiate at sacrificial cere-monies here until 1924. In September of that year, he performed the services for the last time, before following the ex-emperor into exile. In 1931, the French archaeologist and engineer, Georges Bouillard, noted that the wooden altar and the five precious objects needed for the rites were still in place. The hall, however, and its surroundings were already in a parlous state. He wrote of 'falling roofs, broken tiles and a state of decay so great that it is doubtful whether it can ever be reversed'. When one looks at the bright paintwork and tidy terraces today, it is hard to recognize the build-ing in photographs from that time. For a time after restoration it was left empty and the columns could be seen in all their glory; now it acts as a museum for some of the objects found during the excavation of Dingling in the 1950s. The sacrificial hall at Zhao-ling, tomb of the emperor Longqing (who died in 1572) has, however, been restored both inside and out, and there you can see how the original furnishings would have looked.

If you do not have time to visit one of the unrestored tombs as well as Changling, you should continue behind the Hall of Heavenly Favours to the second part of the mausoleum. You can either go through the door behind the screen in the north wall and then down a triple staircase with a marble carpet similar to that on the south side of the building, or you can skirt the hall to east or west.

The entrance to the last courtyard is through a triple doorway decorated with green and yellow tiles. In Changling, the facing is recent but in many of the unrestored tombs the original tile work has survived: there is a particularly fine example in Qingling with complete panels showing baskets filled with leaves and flowers. This use of glazed tiles for decoration in palace architecture was a Ming innovation. Green, yellow, and even black tiles had been mainly used for roofs before this. Under the Ming there was a definite technical improvement in the art of glazing and, for the first time, tiles were baked in five colours to represent the Buddhist five precious jewels. Tiles for imperial use were produced at special potteries in the Western Hills near Beijing and, later, in the mountains near Shenyang, and it became popular to use tiles to decorate walls, door and gate panels, and other flat surfaces such as the sides of the stone foundations of buildings.

The last courtyard is dominated by the stele tower, a square grey stone fortification bearing a red walled pavilion housing the memorial stele to Yongle. The enclosure is short, emphasizing the height of the tower, and the atmosphere is very different from that in the previous courtyard. This is a sombre place, bringing home the proximity of the dead. There are no flower-beds, no ornamental trees, only evergreens providing sustenance for the spirit of the deceased. Inside the triple ceramic doorway is a brightly painted screen-door protecting the direct access to the tomb. (Although the wooden doors have perished in many of the later tombs, the stone framework of this elegant structure has survived in nearly all of them.) The *qilin* on guard on top of the stone posts are similar to but smaller than those on the great *hua biao* columns in the spirit road.

Beneath the tower stands a stone altar with stone replicas of the five precious objects used in the rites. As has been seen above, the sacrifices were always held in the Hall of Heavenly Favours and this altar was a symbolical reminder of prehistoric times in which the sacrificial rites were held in the open. Here, once again, was a conscious attempt by the Ming to re-establish a continuous link between their dynasty and the most ancient traditions of the past. The 'set of five', consisting of a pair of candlesticks, a pair of vases and an incense-burner, were the same as the wooden, lacquer, or *cloisonné* sets used on household altars. The forms of the vases and incense-burner were archaistic—deliberate reproductions of two Bronze Age ritual vessels, the *hu* and the *ding*, whilst the pricket candlestick seems to have come from India (Fig. 3.5). The upper part of the incense-burner shows the dragon moving through clouds above mountains and sea.

3.5 Stone incense-burner, Changling.

The tower guarding the entrance to the fortified 'heavenly' part of the tomb is exactly like a city gate tower. To either side stretch the circular ramparts protecting the grave area with its undergound chamber and the coffin of the deceased emperor. Through its centre is a tunnel which rises steeply, branching to east and west and bringing you out onto the ramparts. Firmly placed on the tower is a red walled pavilion with four arches, only the northern and southern of which are open. Within stands the memorial stele to Yongle. Unlike the memorial stele in the spirit road with its tortoise base, these grave stelae had square or rectangular bases of several layers of stone. As the dynasty progressed, the decoration of these bases became increasingly elaborate but here the slabs are plain. The top of the stele is carved with two dragons among clouds and two large characters in square Han style (*zhuan*) script: *Da Ming* (the Great Ming). The inscription on the body of the stele, which still bears traces of red paint, reads: 'Tomb of the accomplished emperor Chengzu'. (As well as a family name and a reign name, the emperor was given a tomb name after death.)

The fortified enclosure of this tomb is much the largest in the valley. In keeping with its role of symbolizing heaven, it is an almost perfect circle. The ramparts are 3 metres wide and the way round the mound over a kilometre long. Within the ramparts the man-made tumulus rises like a natural hill with a small conical peak in the north-eastern part. The mound is grassy and planted with thujas and oaks. As far as is known, the undergound chamber is intact and here, safe within the grey walls, the great emperor Yongle lies undisturbed.

4
Dingling

DINGLING is the only tomb in the Ming valley which has been excavated. Beside the emperor Wanli (1572–1620) were buried his wife, the empress Xiaoduan, and Xiaojing, an imperial concubine whose son later became emperor. Xiaoduan died in 1620, the same year as the emperor; Xiaojing, who died in 1611, was originally buried in a concubine's tomb and then transferred in 1620 to the imperial mausoleum after her posthumous promotion to empress.

Wanli is a perfect illustration of Lord Acton's dictum that 'power tends to corrupt and absolute power corrupts absolutely'. When he came to the throne at the age of 9, the empire was prosperous. His chief regent was a brilliant administrator and, thanks to tax reforms and the introduction of new crops such as maize and peanuts from North America, both trade and agriculture flourished. However, the young Wanli was confined to the Forbidden City and his education was entrusted to the eunuchs; with unlimited wealth at his disposal and none to gainsay him, he grew up dissolute, extravagant, and lazy. He became so fat that in later years he could not stand unassisted. He neglected affairs of state to such an extent that, at his death, most able men had left government service and retired to the countryside, and more than half the official positions in the provinces were unfilled. In a system imbued with Confucian respect for parents, he offended deeply by staying away from his mother's funeral and refusing to participate in the all-important ancestral rites and sacrifices. In the last twenty-seven years of his reign he only received his senior advisers, the Grand Secretaries, five times, one of which was on his deathbed. For years he remained invisible to his ministers, who received his orders through a filter of eunuchs. Matteo Ricci has described how the great imperial audiences were held without an emperor, visitors kowtowing to an empty throne.

Work on the tomb began in 1585, when the emperor was 22, and lasted for six years; 600,000 men made up the workforce. Characters found on the stone walls indicate that workers were drawn from all over the empire, and that many of them were soldiers. It has been reckoned that the cost, 8 million taels of silver, was equivalent to the entire tax revenue of the state for two years. The emperor showed keen interest in the tomb, visiting it several times during the course of construction and, when it was finished, celebrated the occasion by throwing a large party in the undergound chamber.

Dingling is one of the three-courtyard tombs. It was based on the plans of Yongling and rivalled the scale and splendour of Changling. During the fighting at the fall of the Ming dynasty, most of the surface buildings were destroyed, but these were later rebuilt, albeit on a smaller scale, by the Qing. In 1914, they were again damaged and, today, the only original surface constructions are the walls, the paved terraces, and the great stele tower and pavilion guarding the tomb mound.

The excavations took place from 1956 to 1958 and in the following year Dingling was opened as a public museum. Publication of the results was, however, delayed by the political upheavals of the time. Serious damage was done to some of the finds during the Cultural Revolution; leading members of the excavations were persecuted and many valuable archaeological notes lost. It is only thanks to the dedication, perseverance, and scientific integrity of leading Chinese archaeologists under the late Dr Xia Nai, former Director of the Institute of Archaeology in Beijing, that a scientific report was finally published in 1989.

One of the most difficult tasks in excavating a Chinese tomb is to find the proper entrance. Only in this way can the archaeologists ensure that their entry into the tomb will not disturb its contents. In 1956, work was begun: a 20-metre-deep trench was dug from east to west behind (north of) the stele tower. In the south-west section of the circular ramparts, the diggers found a stone inscribed with three characters: 'Door of the tunnel' (sui dao men); beneath this was a blocked opening in the enclosing wall and a paved way leading towards the centre of the mound. (The stone with the characters, the door, and the paved way can all be seen if you walk round the ramparts in a westerly direction from the stele pavilion.) At the end of the cleared passage, they found, amidst the covering earth, a small stele with the inscription: '16 zhang (52.8m) ahead and 3.5 zhang (11.6m) down from this stele is the wall of the guardian warriors'. When the tomb was finished, these instructions had been left to guide those reopening it for the imperial burial; after Wanli was buried, the stele had simply been forgotten.

It was an incredible stroke of luck, saving months of work. Following the instructions, the archaeologists dug their way to the outer wall of the undergound palace, which was made of bricks. Breaking through this, they found themselves in front of the real entrance—a pair of magnificent marble doors. These doors are replicas of the great gates into the Forbidden City: the nine times nine rows of gilt knobs and fine door handles in the form of an animal head with a ring in its mouth are here reproduced in marble. The doors fitted tightly and were closed with a self-locking mechanism in the interior of the tomb, a stone slab which slid into a niche on the inner side of the doors when they were closed, so that they could not be reopened from the outside. After much experimentation, the archaeologists devised a strong but very thin wire which could be inserted between the doors and looped over the slab; by pushing gently, it was then possible to lower the slab to the ground. After more than three hundred years, the doors, each made from a single block of stone and weighing between 6 and 7

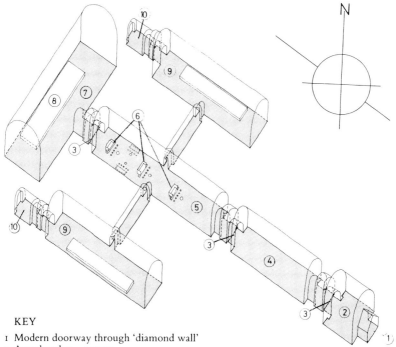

KEY

1 Modern doorway through 'diamond wall'
2 Antechamber—empty
3 Marble doors with self-locking mechanism
4 Outer hall—empty
5 Central hall
6 Three marble thrones, each with five stone bases for ritual vessels and one 'everlasting lamp' (large blue and white vase). Dotted lines show the original positions of the thrones
7 Burial chamber
8 Dais with three coffins (copies) and various smaller chests for treasures (copies)
9 Two side chambers, empty, each with dais for coffin
10 Exit corridors from side chambers

4.1 Undergound chambers, Dingling.

tons, swung open on their marble hinges as if they had been closed the day before. To the archaeologists' delight it became clear that the interior of the tomb had not been disturbed.

Today, the underground chambers are bare of all but their essential furnishings. The most valuable finds are in the Palace Museum in the Forbidden City; replicas of these and a large number of original objects from the tomb are on display in the sacrificial hall at Changling. The underground palace, 27 metres below ground and 84 metres long, consists of six vaulted connecting chambers in the form of a Coptic cross (Fig. 4.1). Between the outer brick wall and the first pair of marble doors is a small antechamber. Within the doors an outer chamber, 20 metres long, 6 metres wide, and 7.2 metres high, leads through a second pair of marble doors to the central hall, which is the same height and width but 32 metres long. Here are three marble thrones, one each for the deceased emperor and his two empresses; in front of each throne is a stone altar with a stone set of the five objects used in the rites, and a large blue and white porcelain vase, originally filled with oil and a wick to provide an 'everlasting lamp' (Fig. 4.2). At the far end of this hall, a third set of marble doors leads into the burial chamber which runs at right angles to the central axis. This, with a floor of finely polished multi-coloured stone, is considerably larger than the previous halls, being 30 metres long, 9 metres wide, and 9.5 metres high. On a stone dais are replicas of the three coffins. Opening off the central hall, to the right and left, a vaulted passage leads to side chambers

4.2 Central undergound chamber with marble thrones, Dingling.

parallel to the central hall. These halls, which are lower than the central three, contained stone coffin platforms but were otherwise empty; they were designed for the burial of empresses who might have outlived the emperor. It would have been considered extremely unlucky to reopen his burial chamber once it had been closed and each side hall was furnished with its own self-locking exit tunnel. The shape of the door openings into these tunnels shows a technical improvement over traditional pre-Ming vaulting methods. Previously, the vaults were rounded, like segments of a circle. Here for the first time they are slightly conical, a form which greatly increased their capacity to bear weight.

Except for bronze beams over the doors, the entire construction is of finely tailored large blocks of white stone. The workmanship was so fine that, even after three centuries, the tomb was completely dry when opened and the everlasting lamps were found to have gone out for lack of oxygen. The area above the doors is carved to imitate a roof; otherwise, the tomb is undecorated, relying for its impact on the simplicity of its lines and the beauty of the stonework.

When the archaeologists opened the doors on 20 October 1957, they found pine boards on the floor with wheel marks on them from the 'dragon hearse' used to transport the heavy coffins. The antechamber and outer hall were empty except for some decayed logs in the latter. (Logs of long-living trees such as thujas were often placed in tombs where their wood was believed to nourish the spirit.) The thrones in the central chamber were arranged differently from their present positions: the emperor's throne faced the entrance, flanked by those of his two consorts. There were still wicks and oil in the everlasting lamps.

All the treasure was placed in the burial chamber at the rear where the three coffins, with the emperor's in the middle, stood on the stone platform. There were objects on and around the coffins and in piles on the platform; more were packed into twenty-nine chests in different parts of the hall. The coffins were similar in size and construction, but that of Xiaojing was of poorer quality. The outer coffins were made of lacquered pine; the inner coffins of fine *nanmu* wood were lacquered inside and out. Around each coffin lay a dozen or more pieces of jade, designed to preserve the body from decay; each piece was inscribed with the name of the stone and its exact weight—in one case 24 kilograms. All three outer coffins were in a bad state but the inner coffins of the emperor and the empress Xiaoduan were relatively intact; that of Xiaojing had disintegrated beyond repair.

45

Inside the inner coffin Wanli's corpse was covered with a brocade quilt beneath which were nine layers of blankets, quilts, and felt pads, one adorned with gold coins marked 'Propitiousness and good fortune'. When the coffin was opened, his long hair was still coiled in a knot under his headdress and secured with long gold hatpins. He was clad in an embroidered burial gown with a jade belt, black gauze cap, yellow damask trousers, and tall boots of plain red satin. The bottom of the coffin was lined with rolls of silk and folded robes; gold and jade objects had been placed above his head and below his feet, and various fabrics, and gold and silver objects, lay at his side.

Xiaoduan, the first empress, was clothed in a yellow-lined jacket embroidered with dragons, a pair of yellow satin lined trousers with embroidered lotuses, a long skirt with dragons on it, and a pair of yellow satin shoes; on her head she wore a pointed black gauze cap decorated with golden hairpins. Her corpse lay between two satin quilts and was supported by four additional quilts onto one of which were sewn one hundred gold coins marked 'Longevity and absence of calamities'. Around her were spare clothes and footwear, daily utensils such as spoons, chopsticks, and bowls, and toilet accessories such as a wash basin, a spouted ewer, and a box of cosmetics all in gold or jade. The second empress, Xiaojing, was similarly arrayed but had two sets of headgear, one which she had worn for her first burial and one which had been placed beside her when she was transferred to Dingling. The earlier headdress was richly decorated with jewels and held in place by bejewelled hatpins. Around her lay many more gold and jewel-studded hatpins and several pairs of earrings. The white jade pendant of one earring was carved in the shape of a hare with a pestle and mortar—the well-known Chinese equivalent of the 'man in the moon' who is pounding the elixir of immortality. The hare's eye, a tiny red garnet less than one millimetre in diameter, had fallen out of its socket and it is recalled that it took hours to find it. Like the first empress, Xiaojing was well provided for daily life and the objects in her coffin included paper money, strings of copper cash from the Wanli period, gold, silver, and bronze jars, plates, bowls, spittoons, and soap dishes.

The area between the inner and outer coffins was filled with blue-and-white and three-coloured porcelain and jade objects. On top of the outer coffins were wooden models of sedan chairs, coaches, spears, bows and arrows, flagstaffs with silk banners, and other items used in imperial processions.

The items found in the burial chamber can be divided into several broad categories: materials and clothing; gold, silver, jade, and be-jewelled ornaments and utensils for the use of the deceased; objects associated with state administration; weapons; porcelain and sets of *mingqi*, or objects made specifically for tomb use. The most valu-able finds, and those which are too fragile to stand exposure, are stored or displayed in the Palace Museum. Most of the remainder are exhibited in the Hall of Heavenly Favours in Changling.

By and large, the three thousand or more objects reflect Wanli's interest in his appearance and in luxurious ornamentation; few items relate to affairs of state. From a historical and scientific point of view, by far the most interesting finds are the silk and clothing. Not only do these display the scope and high technology of Ming silk weaving processes but here, for the first time, we have ex-amples of a complete imperial wardrobe for both sexes. A recurrent theme in the silk and metal objects is that of quality control; far more detailed information is given than that yet required under modern western legislation.

Silk Materials

Over six hundred specimens of silk fabric were found, including damask silk, plain silk, silk gauze, and a kind of brightly coloured brocaded silk known as *zhuang hua*. The process for making the latter, which incorporated tapestry techniques into the weaving, had been used before the Ming but had not previously been applied to silk. One hundred and seventy-seven bolts of silk fabric, 12 to 20 metres long and 72 to 89 centimetres wide, were neatly rolled around cores of straw, folded and tied with three loops of silk thread. Most of these had paper labels recording the colour, pat-tern, material, width, and length; some also specified the name of the material, place of origin, date of weaving, name of the weaver, head of the mill, and supervisor of production. (Most of these bolts came from the official imperial workshops in Nanjing, Suzhou, and Hangzhou.) The principal motifs in the *zhuang hua* and other embroidered fabrics were dragons, phoenixes, other mythological beasts, and ordinary creatures whose names were homophones for auspicious characters such as 'happiness' or 'longevity'. The most common colours were yellow, blue, green, and red. Particularly fine silk embroidery can be seen on two jackets belonging to the empresses with 'the hundred boys pattern'.

Clothing

Some four hundred garments or fragments of garments were found in the coffins. For the emperor, as well as a complete set of under-clothing these included five ceremonial gowns (*gunfu*) of the sort worn at the most important imperial ceremonies in which he paid respects to the ancestors and to heaven, earth, grain, and agriculture. These were embroidered with twelve dragons, the sun, moon, stars, mountains, and pheasants on the back and sleeve; there were also designs of ritual vessels, aquatic plants, rice grains, and weapons, all intended to display the extent of imperial involvement in different fields. With these were a special skirt (*shang*) and apron (*bixi*), worn since ancient times in the important rites. The skirt was of plain yellow silk gauze embroidered with flames, ritual vessels, aquatic plants, rice, and weapons; the apron of red silk gauze with a gauze lining was embroidered with dragons and a flaming pearl. For everyday use, there were sixty-one dragon robes, mostly of woven silk but some of satin or gauze, and several 'lining gowns' of satin, silk, or damask silk. A unique find was a pair of unlined tall boots: the section covering the knees was made of silk tapestry, the leggings were of plain red satin, the insole was of thin leather, whilst the body of the boot consisted of a double layer of coarse white cotton lined with palm fibres stitched together with silk thread and coated with white powder. There were also several ornate headdresses, including one for official audiences, one for travelling, and a black iron helmet decorated with golden warriors and a long red plume.

The clothing of the empresses included over a hundred satin, woven silk, gauze, and velvet gowns embroidered with dragons, phoenixes, flowers, and auspicious characters. Two different types of fastenings—silk loops and gold or gilt bronze buttons—were often used on the same garment. There are beautiful lined, unlined, and cotton padded jackets, skirts, trousers, shoes and socks, and a split cape unlike any other yet seen. Again the footwear disclosed a unique discovery: the only pair of high-heeled shoes known from the Ming dynasty. The insteps are of darkly figured satin, the upper parts embroidered with lotus, pine, and bamboo; the heels are made of several layers of thick straw paper sewn together with silk thread and wrapped in plain red satin. The most spectacular items in the wardrobes of the empresses were their headdresses. Four 'phoenix crowns' were found, the most ornate of which is embroidered with 5,449 pearls; it weighs nearly 3 kilograms (Fig. 4.3). The crowns are a piercing light blue; originally, the upper part was made from kingfisher feathers mounted on paper. Bejewelled dra-

4.3 Phoenix headdress found in the coffin of an empress, Dingling.

gons and phoenixes disport against a background of pale blue enamel clouds and there are long pearl-studded streamers with wings. Both empresses had large quantities of elaborate jewel-studded gold hatpins and beautiful earrings, one of which includes a jade figure surmounted by a little gold Buddha. A variety of jade and gold-ornamented belts and belt hooks were also found.

Gold, Jade, and Bejewelled Objects

Examples in gold were found of all kinds of articles: gold chopsticks and spoons, bowls, pitchers, wash-basins, and wine cups. Each bears the date of manufacture, the name of the object, the quality and weight of the material, and the names of the artisan, the supervisor, and the imperial workshop in which it was made. There are over one hundred ingots of tribute gold marked with similarly detailed information. In a curious reversal of real life, there are a quantity of gold imitations of different coins in use throughout the empire. One of the more extraordinary jade objects is an elegant ewer carved in one piece with a chain joining it to the lid. There are several sets of jade pendants which were hung from the belt in order to make a melodious sound when the wearer moved.

49

Porcelain

The porcelain found consisted mostly of blue-and-white 'plum blossom' porcelain and highly coloured 'three-coloured' ware, including an elaborate incense-burner.

Weapons

Wanli was not a military enthusiast and the military articles were all found in one chest. Apart from the iron helmet mentioned above, the finds included a coat of iron armour, gilt-inlaid swords, spears, and bows and arrows with iron tips.

Mingqi and Objects Relating to the Administration

Compared to tomb finds from earlier dynasties, there were only a few objects relating to the administration and this reflects Wanli's lack of interest in affairs of state. Apart from the ritual clothing and ornaments mentioned above, there were some wooden imperial seals, moulds for making coins, jade emblems of sovereignty, and wooden strips with inscriptions eulogizing the emperor. Typical *mingqi* were the wooden processional objects found on the coffins, a box of over 200 miniature pewter vessels each marked with its name and six boxes of small wooden figures, very simply carved, flat at the back but with clearly recognizable headgear indicating their occupation: officials, servants, cooks, etc.

★ ★ ★

Taken together, these finds provide a valuable glimpse into life in the imperial court in the seventeenth century. The collection of textiles and clothing is unique and has greatly enlarged the scope of our knowledge about Ming techniques in silk weaving and embroidery.

5

The Other Tombs in the Valley

THE remaining mausolea range from Zhaoling, which is being completely restored, to Siling, the tomb of the last Ming emperor, of which virtually nothing has survived. Each of these tombs has its own character and points of interest and, if you can spare the time, it is well worth making the effort to see at least one of them. If you have a whole day, take a picnic: visit Changling, and possibly Dingling, in the morning; then relax in one of the unrestored tombs. Wander at leisure through the peaceful courtyards, examine the marble balusters lying among the wild flowers, study the remnants of walls in the sacrificial halls and the roof structure on gateways or on the stele pavilion, look for the stone drain grids in the courtyards or the water spouts on the outer walls. Above all, enjoy the walk round the ramparts (colour plate 16). These walks are a delight. The circular way leads upwards towards the mountains with their beckoning valleys and overlapping peaks; in the distance, you can see the roofs of other mausolea towering above the evergreen trees on the funeral mounds. Here you are made aware of the history and significance of the tombs in a way which is not possible in the more populated parts of the valley.

The tombs lie along the northern foothills and since the mountains form a curved screen, the tombs on the east and west flanks lie on an almost east–west axis. The second and third tombs were placed to the west and east of Changling. The next four follow each other to the west, Kangling being in the far north-west corner of the valley across a wide river. Between the second and fourth tomb lies the eleventh tomb, Qingling. The reason for this anomaly is that the emperor Taichang, who is buried here, died within a month of ascending the throne. He had not had time to build his Longevity Mausoleum and since it would have been unseemly to keep him unburied for the time needed to construct one, he was buried in a tomb which had been prepared for another emperor, Jingtai, who is buried in a princely tomb in the Western Hills. (When, in 1449, the emperor Zhengtong was taken captive by the Mongols, his younger brother, Jingtai, assumed the title. After Zhengtong's release, he refused to relinquish the throne, keeping Zhengtong a virtual prisoner. Finally, in 1457, Zhengtong ousted Jingtai during a palace coup and he then decreed that the usurper should be denied burial in the dynastic grave area and that his tomb should be razed.

It seems likely that only the surface buildings were destroyed since this was the tomb used for Taichang in 1620.) The *fengshui* in this part of the valley must have been unusual as both this tomb and Xianling next to it have split sites: the first and second courtyards are separated by hills of presumably auspicious shapes and the way between the two parts of the tomb is long and winding.

The eighth tomb, Yongling, broke new ground (colour plate 13). The emperor Jiajing was descended from a younger branch of the family and, whilst accepting the general principle of a single dynastic burial ground, was determined to leave his mark on the valley. He increased the splendour of the spirit road by adding the *pai lou* and the four *hua biao* columns round the stele pavilion. He emphasized that he was starting a new line by choosing a central site, south-east of Changling, and by building a tomb to rival that of Yongle. His successors' tombs, Zhaoling and Dingling, face him on the south-west, and the only other tomb in the east is the twelfth one, Deling, which has a beautiful site looking west across the valley. In winter, the ruined entrance gates frame the setting sun.

A series of concubine graveyards were placed along the western foothills south of Zhaoling and it is here that the last emperor was buried in Siling.

The valley is on a migratory route from northern Siberia and is a good place to watch birds. The area is especially rich in migratory raptors and in winter the reservoir attracts many different species of wildfowl. The courtyards of the unrestored tombs are often filled with pine trees; the tumuli are thickly planted with ancient thujas and large-leaved oaks, and these trees provide shelter and food for thrushes, buntings, and finches. You can often see the Red-billed Blue Magpie with its beautiful long tail; Red-footed Falcons nest in the pines at Kangling and from the stele tower of that tomb you can see Broad-billed Rollers. Other species which nest here are the Eastern Rock-pigeon, the Hoopoe, the Grey-headed Woodpecker, the Red-rumped Swallow and the Chough. For most of the year, the courtyards and tomb mounds are covered with wild flowers. The first to arrive are violets, wild iris, and anemones; then bluebells, small orange lilies, honeysuckle, wild raspberries, and the occasional fritillary; in autumn, there are clusters of wild pink chrysanthemums and pale mauve asters and everywhere, by the bridges and roadside, the sweet mint-like Artemissia.

Owing to the traditionalism of Chinese architecture, there is little if any chronological development in the plan or style of these buildings spanning two and a half centuries, and the best clue to dating is given by the drainage system, which becomes increasingly elaborate. The tombs are described in detail in my *The Imperial Ming Tombs* and, except for the restoration of Zhaoling in the late 1980s and the replanting of some funeral mounds, their state has changed little in the last ten years. The following brief comments are therefore confined to salient points of interest.

Xianling, Tomb of Hongxi (1424–5)

The road runs between the tortoise stele and the first courtyard, which is completely overgrown with pine trees. The two courtyards are separated by a small hill.

Jingling, Tomb of Xuande (1425–35)

The halls and connecting courtyard walls have been cleared away, leaving a set of restored gates and an excellent example of the protective screen in front of the stele tower.

Yuling, Tomb of Zhengtong (1435–49, 1457–64)

Here, and at Maoling, the walls of the sacrificial halls have survived and you can see the foundation stones and ventilation holes for the supporting beams (colour plate 14). Both sets of courtyards are filled with pines and are good places for birds. Four marble basins in the second courtyard were used to contain water.

Maoling, Tomb of Chenghua (1464–87)

The tunnel through the stele tower has been unblocked here, and you can walk straight through to the funeral mound (see Fig. 1.5). The area behind the stele tower is particularly fine with a well-preserved double ramp leading down from the ramparts (see Fig. 1.6) and a free-standing ceramic screen at the southern end of the mound. The thujas on the tumulus are amongst the oldest in the valley.

Tailing, Tomb of Hongzhi (1487–1505)

Apart from Changling, this is the only tomb in which one of the small sacrificial ovens has survived, albeit without its ceramic facing.

Kangling, Tomb of Zhengde (1505–21)

Large parts of the courtyard walls have disappeared and the chief attraction of this tomb is its site. A variety of birds nest here and the walk around the ramparts is of unusual beauty.

Yongling, Tomb of Jiajing (1521–67)

Jiajing designed a tomb which would be fitting for the founder of a new branch of the dynasty and this is one of the most beautiful of all the Ming Tombs (colour plate 13). (The previous emperor had no sons and to find a successor it had been necessary to go back two generations to the line stemming from the emperor Chenghua and his concubine Lady Shao.) Construction started in 1536 and lasted three years. The ground plan follows more closely the idea of the square and the circle than any other tomb and its three courtyards are wider than those of Changling. The entire tomb was originally enclosed by an outer wall making it easily the largest complex in the valley. Whereas the ramparts and stele tower of all the other tombs are made of tailored but unpolished grey stone, those of Yongling are of fine pinky-red polished stone with coloured veins (*hua ban shi* from Feng Shan, Hebei). Instead of the usual tunnel through the stele tower, a pair of wide staircase ramps with crenellated balustrades lead up to the ramparts on either side of the tower. Wanli's Dingling was based on Yongling and the stele pavilions on the stele towers of both are made of stone rather than the customary wooden-beamed structure. (The stone floor of the underground coffin chamber at Dingling is made of the same coloured stone as the Yongling ramparts.)

The sculptural decoration is the finest in the valley. The courtyard halls have been cleared away, revealing the full splendour of the terraces with their elegant stone gargoyles. There are five staircases on the southern side of the terraces, three central and two at the corners for the use of lesser personnel. For the first time, the phoenix appears on the marble stair carpet, playing with the dragon. A lovely lace-barked pine (*Pinus bungeana*) grows in the corner of the first terrace.

Zhaoling, Tomb of Longqing (1567–72)

A new road leads to Zhaoling, branching left from the main road through the valley, after the Dragon and Phoenix Gate, but you can still reach it by the old footpath through the fields from Dingling.

5.1 Hall of Heavenly Favours, Zhaoling, restored 1989.

The decision to restore this tomb was taken in 1985 and work started in 1987. By the autumn of 1989, the approach to the tomb, the pavilion over the tortoise stele and the beautiful triple bridge leading to the main entrance had been repaired. The entrance gate and sacrificial hall had been rebuilt but work on the interior of the hall was still in progress (Fig. 5.1). Some of the original plans for the buildings had been found and, as far as possible, the construction has been carried out as it would have been in the Ming dynasty, using, for example, only wooden nails. The supporting beams for the hall were brought from Colorado in the United States of America. (A stele outside the main entrance commemorates the restoration and expresses gratitude for American help.) The painted decoration on the woodwork is based on original Ming designs found in the Forbidden City and conforms to the original colours of blue, green, and gold. The stone carving was done by workers brought from Chuyang, a village some hundred kilometres from Beijing which has been famous for its sculptors since the Qin and Han dynasties. (Classical sculpture was a hereditary occupation in China and certain villages, even regions, are famous for their skill; their inhabitants were summoned over long distances to carry out work on important buildings.)

The interior of the sacrificial hall is being reconstructed in detail. Facing south are four thrones, one each for the emperor and his three empresses; in front of these are small red wooden footstools. Each throne has an altar in front of it, painted red, and in front of these are lower tables on which the sacrificial offerings were placed.

One is divided into three compartments for holding beef, pork, and lamb. Along the west wall are stands for bronze and stone musical instruments similar to those found in Bronze Age tombs. (It was maintained by those in charge of the rites in imperial times that the use of such instruments and the notes played had been handed down from this epoque.) The area behind the thrones is enclosed by an open-work wooden trellis screen to form a rectangular room divided into small compartments, each with a beautifully decorated very small four-poster bed and quilted covers. Here, hidden from the gaze of those in the hall, the soul could relax whilst watching the rituals being performed in its benefit.

When the work is finished, Zhaoling and Dingling will between them provide a complete picture, above and below, of an imperial Ming tomb.

Qingling, Tomb of Taichang (1620)

As explained above, this is a tomb in which the subterranean section predates the surface buildings by 170 years. The two courtyards are separated by a hill and the way between them leads over a triple bridge and then winds upwards through an orchard of persimmons. The ramparts are very fine, with large sections complete on both sides, and one of the stone gates which led from the ramparts has survived (Fig. 5.2).

5.2 Stone gate by the opening leading from the ramparts into the funeral mound, Qingling.

Deling, Tomb of Tianqi (1620–7)

The site of Deling provides a perfect illustration of *fengshui* and the tomb nestles in a cradle of mountains in the north-east corner of the valley. There is an excellent tortoise stele with a turtle, a crab, a prawn, and a fish carved in the four corners of the base. On the marble carpet leading to the sacrificial hall terrace the dragon has, unusually, caught the pearl. The base of the tomb stele is decorated with Buddhist symbols instead of the customary dragons (see Fig. 1.4).

Siling, Tomb of Chongzhen (1627–44)

Siling is for the romantic with time to spare. The fate of the last emperor, Chongzhen, who hanged himself from a locust tree on Coal Hill as Beijing fell, seems to linger in the air.

The emperor was given a hurried burial in the tomb of an imperial concubine. Later, the Qing provided the tomb with appropriate surface constructions but it was still a modest affair. All that remains is the tumulus (only 4 metres high), some marble stelae, the stone altar, and the altar objects. About a hundred metres further south are two stelae on the grave of Wang Chengen, a faithful eunuch, who remained with the emperor until the end, choosing the same form of death. The altar in front of the imperial tomb mound is carved like a Qing scroll table with upturned ends and the stone 'set of five' stand, not on the altar, but on separate stone tables in front of it. Their decoration is ornate, resembling that on Qing enamel and *cloisonné* objects. This is the only place in the whole valley where sculptural decoration includes real people, animals, or plants. Everywhere else it is confined to stylized geometric or repeating patterns such as lotus petal, waves, or thunder and to fabulous beasts in their supposed habitat of clouds, mountains, and sea.

Concubine Cemeteries

Concubines were buried in special walled enclosures of which the best preserved are west and south-west of Zhaoling. Some of the tomb mounds have clearly been robbed; apart from some stone altars, little else has survived.

6
Administration and Ritual Sacrifices

THE dual functions of the tombs were dealt with by the two arms of government: the task of protecting the graves was entrusted to the military and that of satisfying the spirit through the sacrifices, to the civil authorities.

Responsibility for the defence of the area and, in particular, for keeping marauders out of the imperial burial grounds was entrusted to seven thousand troops under a general, who were housed in a large military headquarters at Changping, just outside the tombs. Smaller detachments were stationed at each tomb, guarding the precincts and patrolling the ramparts. The high red wall adjoining the Great Red Gate enclosed the southern end of the valley; mountain passes were also walled but the rest of the mountain boundary was marked with coloured posts. Penalties for trespassing were dire; the whole valley was a sacred area for the dead.

The civil administration was more complicated. Responsibility was divided between the Imperial Ministry of Works and the Board of Rites. The system was bedevilled by bureaucratic red tape with a multitude of decrees specifying the exact role and rank of the different officials involved. There was an office for the Inspectorate outside each tomb on the east and the main office for the whole valley was next to Changling. The officials were responsible for keeping the tombs in good repair, cultivating the orchards attached to each tomb, and producing all that was needed for the sacrifices. Each tomb was provided with 'guardian families' who lived in a village at the tomb gates. These villages, some of which are still walled, have survived and are known by the name of the tomb to which they belong. (The custom of resettling families on imperial tombs dates back at least to the Han dynasty: 10,000 people were forced to move to the tombs of the first two Han emperors.) The lot of such guardians was not enviable. They were forbidden to till the soil, to hunt, or to fell timber. They were responsible for planting trees—the whole valley was forested—but were only paid when a tree had survived for three years. Worst of all, neither they nor any of their family might be buried in the valley. Their corpses had to be taken out through a special gate and buried outside the walls.

The dates of the sacrifices were fixed by imperial edict. The rites were usually performed on the anniversary of the birth and death of each emperor and empress in the valley, the winter solstice (21

December), the Lantern Festival (15 July), when lanterns were lit to guide wandering spirits home, and the all-important Festival of Pure Brightness (*qing ming*) on 5 April when all Chinese swept the graves of their ancestors and provided them with food. In 1536, the emperor Jiajing abolished the Lantern Festival, which fell in the rainy season, and substituted 23 October, the Day of Frost's Descent, when the ordinary people burned paper clothing at the tombs of their ancestors to keep them warm during the winter. These major ceremonies were carried out by a prince of the first rank, an imperial son-in-law or even the emperor himself. In 1538, whilst his mausoleum was being constructed, the emperor Jiajing performed the rites in the valley three times. Lesser services, conducted by local officials, were held at the full and new moon of each month.

The arrival of imperial delegations imposed a serious burden on the local population, who were responsible for their maintenance, and there are frequent requests in the local records for tax relief. The emperor, with his retinue of over a thousand men, spent one night by the River Sha; the next night he lodged at Changping, rising before dawn and making his way to the robing hall inside the Great Red Gate. Riding within the burial grounds was forbidden so the procession then proceeded on foot or in palanquin. Within the sacrificial hall, the set of five precious objects stood on the altar table, which was painted red. Above the altar hung a tablet with the name of the deceased emperor. This tablet was the heart of the temple and embodied the spirit of the deceased. Outside on the terrace were two incense-burners, two cranes symbolizing longevity, and two deer, all in bronze. We have no descriptions of the services in Ming times but a French officer stationed at the Western Tombs of the Qing dynasty after the Boxer Rising in 1901 had the rare chance for a European of being present at the rites and has given us a detailed description. Whilst the actual dishes may have been different from those offered under the Ming, it seems likely that the general approach was similar. The preparation and slaughter of the animals, a whole ox and two sheep in this case, followed strict rules, and the dishes offered were all subject to regulations: it was, for example, laid down which ranks could eat which of twenty different sorts of biscuits distinguished by their colour. The slaughterhouses and kitchens in which the offerings were prepared were in low side buildings flanking the first courtyard of each tomb. Here also were stored the ritual vessels, archaistic reproductions of vessels used for sacrificial rituals in the Bronze Age.

The main ceremony consisted of three parts. First, a ritual cup of tea in a silver cup was presented to the deceased emperor. The chief authority, the emperor or his substitute, then ceremonially placed incense in the large incense-burner on the altar table whilst another high official poured rice wine into a silver goblet (formed like a Shang dynasty *jue*) and placed this in front of the shrine. Finally came the sending of the visiting card, designed to remind the spirit who was attending to his needs and who should therefore be rewarded. A card with the names of the ruling emperor, empresses, and princes was brought to the altar where the names were read aloud. The officiating personage then knelt three times and kowtowed nine times to his ancestor, whilst the visiting card and a long narrow box containing a roll of silk were taken to the sacrificial ovens and burned. When the senior person had left, the food was distributed to those who had attended the services.

Epilogue

THE Valley of the Thirteen Tombs is one of the great archaeological sites of the world. Situated *en route* between Beijing and the Great Wall, it is one of the most popular tourist attractions in China and, as the years pass, it is likely that both its tourist potential and its scientific interest will be enhanced. Plans are afoot to restore the buildings of another mausoleum and there is little doubt that, sooner or later, another of the great underground palaces will be excavated, providing further insight into the customs, technical skills, and artistic achievements of the Ming dynasty. The popularity of the site brings its perils but experience so far gives good ground for hoping that the valley will absorb these changes without losing its essential character.

Its inherent strength lies in features which cannot be changed. No modernization can alter the shape of the valley with its perfect illustration of the best principles of *fengshui*. Nothing can silence the message expressed by the arrangement of the tomb monuments nor detract from the intrinsic interest of the early fifteenth-century sculptures and the unique collection of Ming architecture. In one way, the valley can be seen as a museum, but it is more than this. It is a place in which history is alive, in which the visitor is consciously aware of the past living on into the present. The judgement of the great Dutch sinologist, Jan Jakob Maria de Groot, is as true today as it was when written a hundred years ago:

The Ming tombs in Ch'ang-p'ing undoubtedly formed one of the largest and most gorgeous royal cemeteries ever laid out by the hand of man. They yield the palm to the Egyptian pyramids in point of bulk, but certainly not in that of style and grandeur.

Appendix

Historical Data

A. MING EMPERORS AND THEIR TOMBS

Family Name	Reign Name	Reign Dates	Tomb
Zhu Chuyi (Zhu Yuanzhang's grandfather)*			Zuling, Lake Hongse, Jiangsu
Zhu Sichen (Zhu Yuanzhang's father)*			Huangling, Anhui
Zhu Yuanzhang	Hongwu	1368–98	Xiaoling, Nanjing
Zhu Yunwen	Jianwen	1398–1402	unknown
Zhu Di	Yongle	1402–24	Changling (1)
Zhu Gaozhi	Hongxi	1424–5	Xianling (2)
Zhu Zhanji	Xuande	1425–35	Jingling (3)
Zhu Qizhen	Zhengtong	1435–49 1457–64	Yuling (4)
Zhu Qiyu	Jingtai	1449–57	Western Hills
Zhu Jianshen	Chenghua	1464–87	Maoling (5)
Zhu Yutang	Hongzhi	1487–1505	Tailing (6)
Zhu Houzhao	Zhengde	1505–21	Kangling (7)
Zhu Houcong	Jiajing	1521–67	Yongling (8)
Zhu Youyuan (Zhu Houcong's father)*			Xianling, Hubei
Zhu Zaihou	Longqing	1567–72	Zhaoling (9)
Zhu Yizhun	Wanli	1572–1620	Dingling (10)
Zhu Changle	Taichang	1620	Qingling (11)
Zhu Yujiao	Tianqi	1620–7	Deling (12)
Zhu Yujian	Chongzhen	1627–44	Siling (13)

*Posthumously raised to imperial rank.

Note: The figures in brackets after the name of each tomb indicate the position of the tomb in the Valley of the Ming Tombs (see endpaper maps).

B. CHRONOLOGICAL TABLE

Shang	c.1550–1027 BC
Zhou	1027–221 BC
Qin	221–206 BC
Western Han	206 BC–AD 24
Eastern Han	25–221
Three Kingdoms	220–280
Western Jin	265–316
Eastern Jin	317–420
Southern Dynasties	420–589
Northern Dynasties	386–581
Sui	581–618
Tang	618–907
Five Dynasties	907–960
Song	960–1279
Jin	1115–1234
Yuan (Mongol)	1271–1368
Ming	1368–1644
Qing	1644–1911
Republic of China	1911–49
People's Republic of China	1949–

Glossary

Ba xia 霸下. Tortoise-like son of the dragon used as a base for memorial tablets.

Fengshui 風水. Ancient theory of geomancy used to determine auspicious sites.

Hua biao 華表. Column signalling the presence of an important monument or gateway.

Li 螭. Hornless dragon.

Ling en dian 祾恩殿. Hall of Heavenly Favours (sacrificial hall).

Ling en men 祾恩門. Gate of Heavenly Favours.

Ling xing men 欞星門. Free-standing gate designed to thwart evil spirits.

Long 龍. Five-clawed dragon.

Makara 摩竭魚. Fabulous beast symbolizing fertility.

Mang 蟒. Four-clawed dragon.

Pai lou 牌樓. Ceremonial or memorial archway.

Qilin 麒麟. Fabulous beast symbolizing good government and peace.

Qiwen 麒吻. Animal head holding upper roof beam in its mouth.

Xiezhi 獬豸. Fabulous beast symbolizing justice.

Zhuan 篆. Form of official script used in the Han dynasty.

Bibliography

A. Non-Chinese Works

Bouillard, Georges. *Les Tombeaux impériaux Ming et Ts'ing*, Beijing, Nachbauer, 1931.

Bouillard, Georges and Commandant Vaudescal. 'Les Sépultures impériales des Ming (Che-San Ling)', *Bulletin de l'École Française de l'Extrême-Orient* (Hanoi), 3(1920).

Cameron, Nigel, *Peking: A Tale of Three Cities*, New York and Tokyo, Weatherhill, 1971.

Cammann, Schuyler. 'Some Strange Ming Beasts', *Oriental Art*, new series 2 (1956): 94–102.

Chow, H.F. 'The Familiar Trees of Hopei', *Peking Natural History Bulletin*, Beijing, 1934.

Combaz, Gisbert. *Sépultures impériales de la Chine*, Brussels, Presses de Vromant, 1907.

de Groot, Jan Jakob Maria. *The Religious System of China*, 6 vols., Leyden, 1892–1910. Reprint of 1892 ed., Taipeh, Ch'eng-wen Publishing Co., 1967.

Fonssagrives, E. *Siling, étude sur les tombeaux de l'ouest de le dynastie des Ts'ing*, Paris, Leroux, 1907.

Garvard, H.S.D. 'Wild Flowers of Northern China and Southern Manchuria', *Peking Natural History Bulletin*, Beijing, 1937.

Goodrich, L. Carrington and Fang Chaoying (eds.), *Dictionary of Ming Biography*, 2 vols., New York and London, Columbia University Press, 1976.

Imbault-Huart, Camille. 'Tombeaux des Ming près de Pékin', *T'oung Pao* (Leyden), No. 4 (1893): 391–401.

Johnston, Reginald F. *Twilight in the Forbidden City*, London, Gollancz, 1934. Reprint: Hong Kong, Oxford University Press, 1985, paperback ed., 1987.

Liang Ssu-ch'eng. *A Pictorial History of Chinese Architecture* (ed. Wilma Fairbank), Cambridge, Mass., Massachusetts Institute of Technology, 1984.

Little, Mrs Archibald. *Round About My Peking Garden*, London, Fisher and Unwin, 1905.

Paludan, Ann. *The Imperial Ming Tombs*, New Haven, Yale University Press and Hong Kong, Hong Kong University Press, 1981.

———. 'The Chinese Spirit Road, Part III: Symbolism and Atrophy', *Orientations* 3(1990): 56-66.

———. *The Chinese Spirit Road: The Classical Tradition of Stone Tomb Statuary*, New Haven, Yale University Press, 1991.

Pirazzoli t'Serstevens, Michèle. *Chine: architecture universelle*. Fribourg, Office du Livre, 1970.

Qiao Yun and Sun Dazhang (eds). *Classical Chinese Architecture*, Hong Kong, Joint Publishing Co., 1986.

Segalen, Victor. *Chine: la grande statuaire*, Paris, Flammarion, 1972. Translated into English by Eleanor Levieux: *The Great Statuary of China*, Chicago and London, University of Chicago Press, 1978.

B. Chinese Works

Dingling, Beijing, Beijing Publishing House, 1973.

Ming Shisanling (The Ming Thirteen Tombs), Beijing, Beijing Publishing House, 1978.

Wang Yan. 'Ming Shisanling bianqiang shankou chakan ji' (Notes on an Investigation into the Perimeter, Walls and Mountain Passes of the Ming Thirteen Tombs), *Kaogu*, 9(1983): 810–16.

——. *Dingling Duo Ying (The Royal Treasury of Dingling: Imperial Ming Tomb)*, 2 vols., Beijing, Cultural Relics Publishing House, 1989.

Index

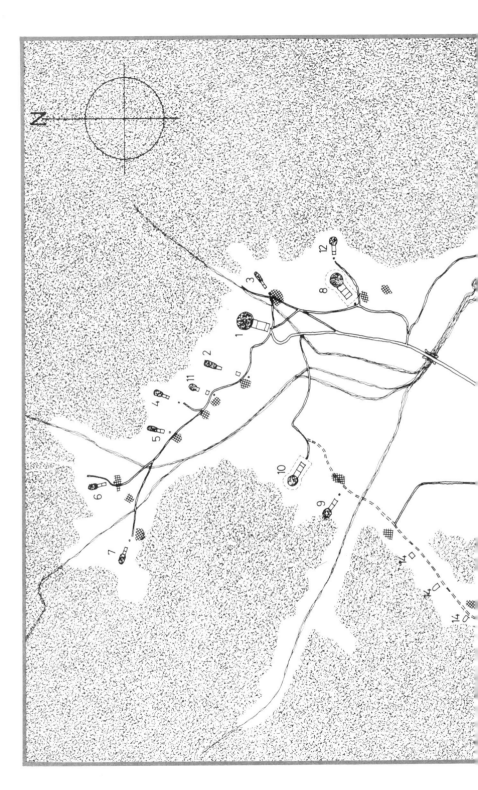